Edith Oenone Somerville (1858–1949) grew up at Drishane, County Cork, Ireland. She belonged to the innermost circle of Anglo-Irish society, and appropriately she shared its interests, particularly its cult of fox-hunting. But her leanings were always towards the arts. After a private education at home she studied art in Düsseldorf, Paris and London, and began her career as an illustrator. Though, after her meeting with her cousin, Violet Martin, in 1886, and the beginning of their long collaboration, she was best known as a writer.

Violet Florence Martin (1862–1915) was born at Ross House, County Galway, Ireland. She took her pseudonym, 'Ross' from her native place. She was educated first by governesses at home, and then at Alexandra College, Dublin. She was an ardent suffragist, and was vice-president of the Munster Women's Franchise League. In 1898, Violet Martin was severely injured in a riding accident, which resulted in several years of invalidism, and which may have contributed to her early death.

Somerville and Ross lived together for most of their lives at the Somerville home in County Cork. They travelled a great deal together in Europe, and spent months at a time in Paris. Separately and together, they wrote some thirty books, mainly set in Ireland, as well as many articles, letters, diaries and jottings. Their first collaboration was *An Irish Cousin* (1889) followed by *Through Connemara in a Governess Cart* (1893) a commission from the *Ladies' Pictorial* to do a series of travel articles which would later make up a book. Among their many collaborations, *The Real Charlotte* (1894) was their first serious novel and generally conceded to be their best. Their most popular books, however, were the rollicking *Some Experiences of the Irish R.M.* (1899) and *Further Experiences of the Irish R.M.* (1908), which in print had a success they were never able to duplicate.

When Violet Martin died, Edith Somerville, deeply affected by her cousin's death, said: 'I have known her help and have thankfully received her inspiration. She has gone, but our collaboration is not ended.' She wrote another thirteen books under the name of 'Somerville and Ross'.

E. Œ. SOMERVILLE and V. M. ROSS

THROUGH
CONNEMARA
IN A
GOVERNESS CART

WITH A NEW INTRODUCTION BY
WILLIAM TREVOR

ILLUSTRATED BY W. W. RUSSELL, FROM SKETCHES BY
EDITH Œ. SOMERVILLE

VIRAGO

Published by VIRAGO PRESS Limited 1990
20–23 Mandela Street, Camden Town, London NW1 0HQ

First published by W.H. Allen & Co. Limited 1893
Virago Press edition reproduced from the W.H. Allen & Co. edition

Introduction copyright © William Trevor 1990

*A CIP catalogue record for this title
is available from the British Library*

Printed in Great Britain by Cox and Wyman Ltd, Reading, Berks

THE following pages, with their accompanying illustrations, originally appeared in the columns of "THE LADIES' PICTORIAL," and are here reprinted by permission of the Proprietors.

LIST OF ILLUSTRATIONS.

INTRODUCTION

The descriptive term, Anglo-Irish, is simple in its historical implication. It suggests a foothold within the political ascendancy in Ireland, a continuing connection with England, and a preference for the English language and religion. But when the expression relates purely to literature a confusion is introduced.

Writing in the early 1930s, the scholar and short-story writer Daniel Corkery offered an academic definition that has held sway ever since: 'Literature written in English by Irishmen is now known among us as Anglo-Irish literature, while by Irish literature we mean the literature written in the Irish language and that alone.'

It may seem a little odd that Irishmen such as Frank O'Connor, Liam O'Flaherty and James Joyce should be placed in one category as persons and in another as writers. Nor does there seem to be any good reason why the term 'Irish literature' should not be accepted to mean the writing of Irish people in either Irish or English, and the term 'Anglo-Irish literature' be allowed to designate the writing of the Anglo-Irish. But it is not so.

Scribbling away in one drawing-room or another, Somerville and Ross were Anglo-Irish both as human beings and as fiction writers. They were rooted in its Big House world; its mores and its attitudes were theirs. What they wrote, rather more than what they were, offended Daniel Corkery, and to this day that same offence is regularly given. A dislike of what Corkery called a 'colonial culture' is understandable indeed, but at the same time it cannot be sensibly argued that literature is a national property – that Turgenev, for instance, wrote only 'for Russia' and Ibsen 'for no alien market'. The truth is that art, no matter what its roots, cannot be owned in this way. In the very process of becoming art it also becomes universal.

Somerville and Ross have to be accepted as creatures of their time and class – and if necessary forgiven for it. They can be accused of presenting the quaintness of Irish life as an Irish joke, of patronising the lower orders by imitating their speech and exposing their foibles. It is true that, like Dickens, they did so affectionately and without sarcasm, but Dickens shared his Englishness with Joe Gargery and Sam Weller as much as he did with Miss Havisham and Lady Tippens. Somerville and Ross, although they considered themselves totally Irish, were on trickier terrain.

Edith Oenone Somerville was born in 1858 on the island of Corfu, where her father commanded the 3rd Buffs. When his active military life ended Colonel Thomas Somerville came to live at Drishane in Castletownshend, West Cork – a house and a place associated ever since with the literary talent of his daughter.

Violet Martin, Edith's cousin and four years younger, came of similar stock in County Galway. An ancestor had helped Strongbow to invade Ireland, was granted an estate near Oughterard, and went crusading with Richard Coeur de Lion. In 1777 Ross House, taking its title from the nearby lake, was built where a Martin castle had once stood. When the possibility that Violet's name might appear in print was first mooted it was decided by the family that 'Martin Ross' was a more suitable form for it to take.

Edith was an extrovert, lighthearted girl who loved dogs, enjoyed riding, and painted a bit. Violet, short-sighted and more intense, often permitted a sadness to still her neat, handsome features. The famous collaboration began, not with words on paper nor even stories exchanged, but when Edith painted Violet's portrait in 1886. Attired for the hunting field, Violet perches on the edge of a chair, unsmiling, spectacles dangling, a little melancholy. It isn't difficult to imagine the bustling Edith, hair pinned up, glancing back and forth from canvas to model, chattering, or muttering to herself. Slowly they became friends, and out of the warmth that developed came everything else.

Writing is a solitary business, and to writers who have not engaged in it collaboration is sometimes not easy to understand. 'Our work was done conversationally,' Edith has explained. 'One or the other – not infrequently both simultaneously – would state a proposition. This would be argued, combated perhaps, approved or modified; it would be written down by the (wholly fortuitous) holder of the pen, would be scratched out, scribbled in again.' It is probably true that Violet supplied the sombre tones and the subtler intricacies of plotting, that somewhere in her contribution lay the genius of the partnership. But it is as easy to believe that nothing would have surfaced as completely and as felicitously without Edith's corresponding view of the same scenes and characters, and her meticulous scrutiny of all they invented. The cousins were two halves of a whole, quibbling and enthusing, sharing amazement and delight – two women, one writer. When Violet died Edith continued as if this separation had not occurred, believing in fact that she still received her cousin's guidance and inspiration.

Edith loved Violet in the possessive, passionate manner that caused Ethel Smyth, on a visit to Drishane in 1919, four years after Violet's death, to assume that the pair had been practising lesbians. They had not, of course. As their biographer, Maurice Collis, points out, Violet might have married but Edith would not have cared for the physical attentions of a man. Nor, though, did she care for those of Dame Ethel. The affection that developed between the cousins, more obsessive on Edith's side than on Violet's, found its release in their literary conjunction. For each, in her different way, that was sufficient.

In July 1890, having already published *An Irish Cousin* but still short of funds, they suggested a series of travel articles to the *Ladies' Pictorial*. Edith would illustrate a trip through Connemara which they planned to make in a jennet and trap, hoping for enough amusement and adventure en route to make up a book after the pieces had appeared in the magazine.

'Johnny Flaherty have a nice jinnet,' they were told in Galway. 'She's able to kill any horse on the road.'

Mr Flaherty promised that if they refrained from touching the animal's ears she'd give them no trouble at all, being if anything 'over-anxious for the road'. With this companion – sometimes as eager as her owner declared, but as often reluctant to move in any direction whatsoever – the two set about dawdling through Connemara with their Bath Olivers and their pot of Bovril, their spirit lamp and a folding rubber bath. They were drenched, assaulted by midges, nibbled by fleas, abused by a harridan who didn't like the look of them, made fools of by the jennet. 'Ah, don't be sparin' him that way, ladies,' the natives called out. 'Nourish him wid the whip.'

But from Maam Cross to Recess, by the waters of Inagh and the Pass of Selruck, their trials were rewarded. Nothing was taken for granted: a dog was never just a dog, a house never just a house, there were no mere passers-by. On a dull day they embellished, for above all else Somerville and Ross are storytellers.

'We did not ask the Widow Joyce if she could take us in. We simply walked into the house and stayed there.'

If inconvenience resulted, the Joyce household took it in its stride. After the widow had prepared and served a meal and the time came for retirement, she apologised for the fact that the family would now have to pass through the guests' bedroom in order to mount to the loft above it. '. . . a procession of Joyces slowly filed up the ladder, headed by the younger sons of the house, and followed by the widow and the daughters.'

In the meantime another procession was forming beneath the bedclothes. 'It isn't the little bit they ates I begridges them,' mimicked one of the ladies, 'but 'tis the continial thramplin' they keeps up.' And when the fleas quietened, a goose emerged from beneath the bed.

There is no reference to this overnight stay in the Joyce house in the diaries that were kept. Bits and pieces, experienced elsewhere or by others, may have been knocked together, exaggerated to taste. Or the whole episode may be an invention. *Through Connemara in a Governess Cart* is no strict documentary. Its authors' gifts lie elsewhere: their shared ear for dialect, their shared fascination with the peculiar and the extraordinary, their sense of humour and their clear literary style, combine with an insistent imagination to make them what they so uniquely are.

Within their own Big House realm there was a certain isolation, bred of the suspicion that fiction-writers inspire: thrown together in their governess cart or in the draughty comfort of Drishane, they found the courage to ignore it. And it was isolation again – the very distance that lay between two upper-class women and the Ireland they wrote about – that permitted their talent to breathe and develop. By chance, or accident of birth, they discovered the perspective that art demands.

William Trevor, 1990

THROUGH CONNEMARA IN A GOVERNESS-CART.

CHAPTER I.

MY second cousin and I came to London for ten days in the middle of last June, and we stayed there for three weeks, waiting for a fine day.

We were Irish, and all the English with whom we had hitherto come in contact had impressed upon us that we should never know what fine weather was till we came to England. Perhaps we came at a bad moment, when the weather, like the shops, was having its cheap sales. Certainly such half-hours of sunshine as we came in for were of the nature of " soiled remnants," and at the end of the three weeks aforesaid we began to feel a good deal discouraged. Things came to a climax one day when we had sat for three-quarters of an hour in a Hungarian bread shop in Regent Street, waiting for the rain to clear off enough to let us get down to the New Gallery. As the fifth party of moist ladies came in and propped their dripping umbrellas against the wall behind us, and remarked that they had never *seen* such rain, our resolution first began to take shape.

" Hansom ! " said my second cousin.

" Home ! " said I.

By home, of course we meant the lodgings—the remote, the Bayswaterian, but still, the cheap, the confidential ; for be they never so homely, there's no place—for sluttish comfort and unmolested unpunctuality—like lodgings.

" England is no fit place for a lady to be in," said my second cousin, as we drove away in our hansom with the glass down.

" I'd be ashamed to show such weather to a Connemara pig," I replied.

Now Connemara is a sore subject with my second

cousin, who lives within sight of its mountains, and, as is usually the case, has never explored the glories of her native country, which was why I mentioned Connemara. She generally changes the conversation on these occasions; but this time she looked me steadily in the face and said,

"Well, let's go to Connemara!"

I was so surprised that I inadvertently pressed the indiarubber ball of the whistle on which my hand was resting, and its despairing wail filled the silence like a note of horror.

"Let's get an ass and an ass-car!" said my cousin, relapsing in her excitement into her native idiom, and taking no notice of the fact that the hansom had stopped, and that I was inventing a lie for the driver; "or some sort of a yoke, whatever, and we'll drive through Connemara."

In the seclusion of the back bedroom we reviewed the position, while around us on the lodging-house pegs hung the draggled ghosts of what had been our Sunday dresses.

"That's the thing I wore last night!" said my second cousin, in a hard, flat voice, lifting with loathing finger a soaked flounce. As she did so, the river sand fell from it into the boots that stood beneath.

"Soil of tea-garden, Kingston-on-Thames. Result of boating-picnic that has to fly for refuge to an inn-parlour ten minutes after it has started."

."It will wash," I answered gloomily. "But look at that!" Here I pointed to an evening gown erstwhile, to quote an Irish divine, "the brightest feather in my crown." "That's what comes of trailing through Bow Street after the opera, looking for a hansom during the police riots. Give me Irish weather and the R.I.C.! We *will* go to Connemara!"

. . . . . .

The Milford and Cork boat starts at eight, and at half-past eight a doomed crowd was sitting round its still stationary tea-table. My second cousin was feverishly eating dry toast and drinking a precautionary brandy and soda, but the others were revelling

"IN THE SECLUSION OF THE BACK BEDROOM."

on beefsteak and fried fish. The company was mixed. Opposite to us sat an American and his bride, both young, and both uncertain of the rules that govern the consumption of fish; the bride feeling that a couple of small forks, held as though they were pens, would meet the situation, while her big, red-headed husband evidently believed that by holding the fork in the right hand and the knife in the left the impropriety of using the latter would be condoned. Beside us were two elderly ladies, returning, like us, to their native land.

"Yes, me dear," we heard one saying to the other; "I had nothing only my two big boxes and seven little small parcels, and poor little Charlie's rabbit, and that porther wanted to get thruppence out o' me!"

"D'ye tell me so?" remarked the friend.

"Yes, dear, he did indeed! He wanted thruppence and I gave him tuppence; he was tough, very tough, but I was shtubborn!"

"Ah, them English is great rogues," said the friend, consolingly.

"More fish, Miss?" said the unobservant steward to my second cousin, thrusting a generous helping under her nose. It wanted but that, and she retired to the doubtful security of the ladies' cabin.

We have travelled with many stewardesses on the various routes between England and Cork, and we have found that, as a species, they have at least two great points in common. They are all Irish, and they are all relentlessly conversational. They have no respect for the sanctity of the silence in which the indifferent sailor wishes to shroud herself; it is impossible for them to comprehend those solemn moments, when the thoughts are turned wholly inwards in a tumult of questioning, while the body lies in mummy stillness waiting for what the night shall bring forth. Their leading object seems to be to acquire information, but they are not chary of personal detail, and, speaking from experience, I should say that a stewardess will confide anything to the passenger by whose berth she has elected to take down her hair. For stewardesses generally do their

hair two or three times in the course of a twelve
hours' crossing. When you go on board you find
them at it. Your evening ablutions are embittered
by the discovery of their hair-pins in the soap-dish,
and at earliest dawn the traveller is aware of the
stewardess combing her shining tresses over the
washing-stand. I have sometimes wondered if from
this custom arose the fable that the mermaid,
when not decoying sailors to their fate, is incess-
antly "racking her poll," as they say in the county
Cork.

We will not linger on the details of the night, the
sufferings of little Charlie, who, on the plea of extreme youth, had been imported by his mother into
the ladies' cabin ; the rustlings and chumping of the
rabbit, whose basket occupied the greater part of the
cabin table, or the murmured confidences exchanged
through the night hours by the stewardess and the
friend of Charlie's mother. These things are being
forgotten by us as fast as may be ; but my second
cousin says she never *can* forget the waft of pigs that

came to her through the porthole as the steamer drew alongside of the Cork quay.

The exigencies of return tickets had compelled us to go to Connemara *viâ* Cork and Milford, and it certainly is not the route we would recommend ; however, it has its advantages, and we were vouchsafed a time of precious rest before the starting of our train for Limerick at 2.10, and we reposed in peace on the sofas of the ladies' drawing-room in the Imperial Hotel. Much might be said, were there time, of the demeanour of ladies in hotel drawing-rooms ; so hushed, so self-conscious, so eminent in all those qualities with which they are endued by the artist who "does" the hotel interiors for the guide-books. It is almost possible to believe that they are not engaged for the season to impart tone, and to show how agreeable a lounge life can be when spent in the elegant leisure that is the atmosphere of hotel drawing-rooms.

We crossed Cork on an outside-car ; and here, no doubt, we should enter on a description of its perils

which would convulse and alarm English readers in
the old, old way ; but we may as well own at once
that we know all about outside-cars ; we believe we
went to be christened on an outside-car, and we did
not hold on even then—we certainly have not done so
since.

Let us rather embark on a topic in which all,
saving a besotted few, will sympathise. The nursery
en voyage—the nurse, the nursemaid, the child, the
feeding-bottle. These beset every traveller's path,
and we had considerably more than our fair share of
them between Cork and Limerick. At Cork they
descended upon the train, as it lay replete and helpless, a moment before starting, and before we had
well understood the extent of the calamity, a nurse
was glaring defiance at us over the white bonnet of a
bellowing baby, and a nursemaid was already opening
her basket of food for the benefit of two children of
the dread ages of three and five respectively. Some
rash glance on the part of my second cousin must
have betrayed our sentiments to the nurse, and it is

hard to say which was worse, her exaggerated anxiety to snatch the children from all contact with us, or the imbecile belief of the nursemaid that we wanted to play with them, and, of the two, enjoyed their wiping their hands on our rug in the intervals between the oranges. They never ceased eating oranges, those children. Oranges, seed cake, milk ; these succeeded one another in a sort of vicious circle. An enterprising advertiser asks, "What is more terrible than war?" We answer unhesitatingly, oranges in the hands of young children.

However, everything, even the waits at the stations between Limerick and Athenry, comes to an end if you can live it out, and at about nine o'clock at night we were in Galway. Scarcely by our own volition, we found ourselves in an hotel 'bus, and we were too tired to do more than notice the familiar Galway smell of turf smoke as we bucketted through Eyre Square to our hostelry. It may be as well at this point to seriously assure English readers that the word " peat " is not used in Ireland in reference to fuel by anyone except possibly the Saxon tourist. Let it therefore be accepted that when we say "turf" we mean peat, and when, if ever, we say Pete, we mean the diminutive of Peter, no matter what the spelling.

We breakfasted leisurely and late next morning, serenaded by the screams of pigs, for it was fair day, and the market square was blocked with carts tightly packed with pigs, or bearing tall obelisks of sods of turf, built with Egyptian precision. We cast our eye abroad upon a drove of Connemara ponies, driven in for sale like so many sheep, and my second cousin immediately formed the romantic project of hiring one of these and a small trap for our Connemara expedition.

"They are such hardy little things," she said, enthusiastically, "we had two of them once, and they always lived on grass. Of course they never did any work really, and I remember they used to bite anyone who tried to catch them—but still I think one of them would be just the thing."

" I beg your pardon, Miss," said the waiter, who was taking away our breakfast things, " but thim ponies is very arch for the likes of you to drive. One o' thim'd be apt to lie down in the road with yerself and the thrap, and maybe it'd be dark night before he'd rise up for ye. Faith, there was one o' them was near atin' the face off a cousin o' me own that was enticin' him to stand up out o' the way o' the mail-car."

My second cousin looked furtively at me, and rose from her seat in some confusion.

" Oh, I think we should be able to manage a pony," she said, with a sudden resumption of the dignity that I had noticed she had laid aside since her arrival in Galway. " Is there—er—any two-wheeled—er—trap to be had ? "

" Sure there is, Miss, and a nate little yoke it'd be for the two of ye, though the last time it was out one of the shafts——"

" Is it in the yard ? " interrupted my second cousin, severely.

" It is, Miss, but the step took the ground——"

My cousin here left the room, and I followed her. A few moments later the trap was wheeled into the yard for our inspection. It was apparently a seg-ment of an antediluvian brougham, with a slight flavour about it of a hansom turned the wrong way, though its great-grandfather had probably been a highly-connected sedan-chair. The door was at the back, as in an omnibus, the floor was about six inches above the ground, and the two people whom it with difficulty contained had to sit with their backs to the horse, rocking and swinging between the two immense wheels, of which they had a dizzy prospect through the little side windows.

" There it is for ye, now!" said the waiter, triumphantly. He had followed us downstairs and was negligently polishing a tablespoon with his napkin. "And Jimmy," indicating the ostler, "'ll know of the very horse that'll be fit to put under it."

" No," we said faintly, "that would never do ; we want to drive ourselves."

The ostler fell into an attitude of dramatic meditation.

"Would you be agin dhrivin' a side-car?"

We said "No."

Equally dramatic ecstasy on the part of both ostler and waiter. The former, strange to say, had a friend who was the one person in Galway who had the very thing we wanted. "Letyees be gettin' ready now," said Jimmy, "for I'll go fetch it this minute."

About half an hour later we were standing at the hotel doorsteps, prepared for our trial trip. On the pavement were clustered about us the beggarwomen of Galway—an awesome crew, from whose mouths proceeded an uninterrupted flow of blessings and cursings, the former levelled at us, the latter at each other and the children who hung about their skirts. We pushed our way through them, and getting up on the car announced that we were ready to start, but some delay in obtaining a piece of cord to tie up the breeching gave the beggars a precious opportunity.

My second cousin was recognised, and greeted by name with every endearment.

"Aha! didn't I tell ye 'twas her?" "Arrah, shut yer mouth, Nellie Morris. I knew the fine full eyes of her since she was a baby." "Don't mind them, darlin'," said a deep voice on a level with the step of the car; "sure ye'll give to yer own little Judy from Menlo?"

This was my cousin's own little Judy from Menlo, and at her invocation we both snatched from our purses the necessary blackmail and dispensed it with furious haste. Most people would pay largely to escape from the appalling presence of this seventy-year-old nightmare of two foot nothing, and she is well aware of its compelling power.

The car started with a jerk, the driver boy running by the horse's side till he had goaded it into a trot, and then jumping on the driving-seat he lashed it into a gallop, and we swung out of Eyre Square followed by the admiring screams of the beggars. The pace was kept up, and we were well out of Galway before a slightly perceptible hill suddenly changed it to a funeral crawl—the animal's head disappearing between its forelegs.

"Give me the reins," said my second cousin. 'These country boys never know how to drive," she added in an undertone as she took them from the boy. The horse, a pale yellow creature, with a rusty black mane and tail, turned his head, and fixing a penetrating eye upon her, slightly slackened his pace. My cousin administered a professional flick of the whip, whereon he shrank to the other side of the road, jamming the step of the car against a telegraph post and compelling me to hurriedly whirl my legs up on to the seat. We slurred over the incident, however, and proceeded at the same pace to the top of the hill. A judicious kick from the boy urged the horse into an amble, and things were going on beautifully when we drew near a pool of water by the roadside.

"You see he goes very well when he is properly driven," my second cousin began, leaning noncha-

"IF YE BATE HIM ANY MORE HE'LL LIE DOWN."

lantly across the car towards me. As she spoke, the
car gave a lurch and came to a standstill at the edge
of the pool. Apparently the yellow horse was
thirsty. He was with difficulty dragged into the
middle of the road again, but beyond the pool he
refused to go. The boy got down with the air of one
used to these things.

" If ye bate him any more he'll lie down," he said
to my cousin. " I'll go to the house beyond and
gether a couple o' the neighbours."

The neighbours—that is to say, the whole of
the inhabitants of the house—turned out with en-
thusiasm, and, having put stones behind the wheels,
addressed themselves to the yellow horse with strange
oaths and with many varieties of sticks.

" 'Tis little he cares for yer bating," screamed the
mother after several minutes of struggle. " Let him
dhrink his fill o' the pool and he'll go to America for
ye."

We thought that on the whole we should prefer
to return to Galway, and though assured by the boy

of ultimate victory, we turned and made for the town on foot.

" I scarcely think that horse will do," said my second cousin, after we had walked about half a mile, turning on me a face still purple from her exertions with the whip. " We want a freer animal than that."

She had scarcely finished when there was a thundering on the road behind us, a sound of furious galloping and shouting, and the car appeared in sight, packed with men, and swinging from side to side as the yellow horse came along with a racing stride.

" Ye can sit up on the car now!" called out the boy as they neared us, " he'll go aisy from this out."

The car pulled up, and the volunteers got off it with loud and even devotional assurances of the yellow horse's perfections.

But we walked back to Galway.

CHAPTER II.

SHALL we admit that, after all, the first stage of our journey was accomplished by means of the mail-car? We had been assured, on reliable authority, that Oughterard, fourteen Irish miles from Galway, was the place where we should find what we wanted, and with a dubious faith we climbed the steep side of the mail car, and wedged ourselves between a stout priest and an English tourist. Above us towered the mail baskets, and a miscellaneous pile of luggage, roped together with that ingenuity that necessity has developed in the Irish carman, and crowning all, the patriarchal countenance of a goat looked down upon us in severe amazement from over the rim of an immense hamper.

We have said in our haste that we never hold on on

jaunting-cars, but as the dromedary to the park hack, so is the mail-car to the ordinary "outside" of its species.   It is large enough to hold six people on each side, and is dragged by three horses at a speed that takes no account of ruts and patches of stones and sharp corners, or of the fact that the unstable passenger has nothing to grasp at in time of need, except his equally unstable fellow-traveller.   We held on to the priest and the tourist with all the power of our elbows, and derived at least some moral support from the certainty that when we fell off the car we should, like Samson, carry widespread disaster with us.   But somehow people do not fall off these cars; and even the most unschooled of Saxons sits and swings and bows on the narrow seat with a security that must surprise himself.

An Irish mile is, roughly speaking, a mile and a quarter English, so we leave to the accomplished reader the computation of the distance from Galway to Oughterard according to the rightful standard.   It is not in the ordinary sense a very interesting drive;

the guide-books pass it over in a breath in their haste
to blossom out into the hotels and fisheries of Connemara ; but to the eye that comes fresh to it from the
offensively sleek and primly-partitioned pastures of
England this first impression of Galway and its un-
trammelled bogs and rocks will be as lasting as any
that come after. We ourselves might have framed
many moving sentences about the desolate houses
standing amongst the neglected timber within their
broken demesne walls, but "all our mind was clouded
with a doubt," and from the peculiar protrusion of my
cousin's nether lip, I could gather that her moodiness
was the outward token of an agitated mental parade
of all the Oughterard horseflesh with which she was
acquainted.

We spent that night at Oughterard in Miss Murphy's
comfortable little hotel, and the next morning found
us embarked once more in search of a means of travel.
The trap had been unearthed—the trap of our brightest dreams—a governess-cart that would just hold two
people and a reasonable amount of luggage ; but the

horse was the trouble. Various suggestions had been made : some had been feasible, and the one thing on which we were firmly decided, viz., the governess-cart, seemed an impossibility.

"Well, Miss, ye see, she's only just in off grass ; sure she'll rejoice greatly in the coorse of the next few days, and she'd fit the shafts well enough so."

Thus spoke the proprietor of many flocks and herds to whom we had addressed ourselves. "It's a pity there's nothing would suit ye only the little thrap, but surely ye might thry her whatever."

"She" was a farm mare of mountainous propor-tions, who after violent exertions had been squeezed between the shafts of the governess-cart, and she now stood gazing plaintively at us, and switching her flowing tail, while the shafts made grooves for them-selves in her fat sides.

"Sit in now, Miss, and dhrive her out o' the yard." My second cousin got in with ease, the step of the trap being almost on the ground, owing to the un-natural elevation of its shafts, and the mare strode heavily forward. My cousin clutched the front rail convulsively

"I am slipping out!" she said with a sudden tension in her voice. Had she thought of it she might have held on by the tail, which hung down like a massive bell-rope above her, but as it was, after a moment or two of painful indecision, she made a hurried but safe exit over the door of the trap. The fate of the expedition trembled in the balance, and the group of spectators who had formed round us began to look concerned. The mare was extracted with some difficulty from the pinioning shafts, and all things were as they were, the governess-cart with its shafts on the ground, and my cousin and I with our hearts in our boots, when a voice came to us from the crowd—

"Johnny Flaherty have a nice jinnet."

"A betther never shtud in Galway!" said another voice. "She's able to kill anny horse on the road."

An excited discussion followed, in the course of which it was brought forward as the jennet's strongest

recommendation that she was the daughter of the
lady whose majestic build had lost to us the enjoy-

"SHE'S A LITTLE GIDDY ABOUT THE HEAD, MISS."

ment of her admirable moral qualities.   Finally a portion of the crowd detached itself and ran up the street,
returning in a few minutes with Johnny Flaherty and

a long-legged, long-eared brown animal, which, as it approached, cast an eye of sour suspicion upon us and its mother. There was no doubt but that this creature would fit the trap, but with haunting memories of the iniquities of mules and their like we asked if it was gentle.

"She's a little giddy about the head, Miss," said the owner diffidently ; "but if ye'll not touch the ears she's the quitest little thing at all. Back in, Sibbie ! "

Sibbie backed in with an almost unwholesome docility, and was harnessed in the twinkling of an eye, the lookers-on assisting enthusiastically. She was led out of the yard. We got in with Mr. Flaherty, and before the crowd had time to cross themselves we were out of sight.

"Perfection ! " I gasped, with the wind whistling in my teeth as Sibbie sped like a rat between the shafts that had given her good mother her first insight into tight lacing. "She goes splendidly—the very thing ! but now isn't it time to go back and get in our things ? "

My cousin did not answer ; she was driving, and something told me that the same idea had occurred to her. She was leaning rigidly back, and one of her gloves had burst at the knuckles. Johnny Flaherty extended a large hand and laid it on the reins.

" She's over-anxious for the road," he said apologetically, as he brought the jennet to a standstill ; " but I'll put a curb-chain on her for ye."

We turned and wheeled back into Oughterard, a positive adoration for Sibbie, with her discreet brown quarters and slender, rapier-like legs, welling up in us. Now, thinking over these things, it seems possible that her week's hire approached her net value, but at the time of bargaining we felt that her price was far above rubies.

As this is the record of a genuine expedition, it is perhaps advisable to say that our luggage consisted of a portmanteau, a dressing bag, a well-supplied luncheon basket, and a large and reliable gingham umbrella, purchased for the sum of three shillings in Oughterard. We viewed the elaborate stowing of

"WE VIEWED THE STOWING OF THE GOVERNESS-CART."

these in the governess cart, and then went to Mr. Flaherty for his final sailing orders.

" Ye'll mind her passing Flanigan's ; she have a fashion of running in there ; and as for passing our own place, I have a boy standin' there now in the archway with a stick, the way he'd turn her back out of it if she'd make a dart for the stable, and I'll put a rope in the thrap for fear anything might break on ye."

Mr. Flaherty looked a little anxious as he gave us these directions, and when he had gone for the rope, an old woman, who had been regarding us with a sympathetic solicitude, came up to my cousin and took her by the arm.

" That the Lord may save yees ! that's all I'll say," she groaned ; " if 'twas a horse itself, I'd say nothin', but thim mules is nayther here nor there. Sure asthore, ye couldn't tell the minnit he'd turn into a boghole, when he doesn't know ye, and thim Cunnemarra roads has nothin' before him to shtop him only the grace of God ! and the wather up aich side of the road by yees as deep as a well ! "

It was painful to find that Oughterard credited the jennet with the sole conduct of the expedition, and regarded us as helpless dependents on her will and pleasure. But the old woman's agitation was quite unaffected, and the last thing we heard, as we flourished down the main street, was her voice uplifted in prayerful lamentation.

Owing possibly to the fact that Mr. Flaherty's boy was demonstrating with the pitch-fork in the arch-way leading to the stable, Sibbie made no attempt to "dart" into it as her owner had anticipated, and nothing marred the dignity of our departure. We turned cautiously over the crooked bridge, and drove along beside the river, running black under tall trees, with patches of foam sailing fast on it. Villas with trimly clipped ivy and flower-beds all ablaze were on our other hand, surburban in self-respecting neatness, romantic by force of surroundings and of something old-fashioned and solid in their build.

"This is the best village for its size this side of Galway," said my cousin, with a languid indifference

that, as I well knew, masked the seething self-satisfaction of the resident in the neighbourhood. "And
the place has improved so wonderfully. For instance,
there's the Widow's Almshouse. It isn't so very long

ago since an old woman
said to my grandmother,
'That's the Widdies' Alm-
house, and sorra widdy in
it but one little owld man,'
and now it's simply bursting
with widows—at least, I
mean——"

This remarkable illus-
tration of the prosperity of
Oughterard was suddenly
interrupted. We had for-

"MR. FLAHERTY'S BOY WAS DE-
MONSTRATING WITH A PITCH-
FORK."

gotten that the residence of the too fascinating Mr.
Flanigan was at hand, but not so Sibbie. With the
subtlety of her race, she cloaked her design in a ful-
some submissiveness, as the deadly spirit is sheathed
in the syrup of the liqueur, and turning in full career,

without so much as an indication from her long expressive ears, she made for the gate of which we had been warned. By a special interposition of Providence it was closed, but we were both jerked forward in a very humiliating way, and there was much unseemly hectoring and lashing before we could drag her from the haven where she would be. The seeds of distrust were from that moment sown in our hearts, and we proceeded with a want of confidence that we had never afterwards reason to regret.

A few moments of steep ascent brought us out on to the moor that is the entrance to Connemara ; a wide brown place of heather and bog, with the sinuous shining of the Oughterard river saving it from the suspicion of monotony. The level road ran out in front of us till it dwindled into a white thread, the distant hills were no more than confidential blue hints of what we were to see, the sun shone, the strong west wind made us rejoice that we had stitched elastic into our hats, and the exhilaration of our feelings found vent in one passion-fraught word—luncheon.

A great many people have asked us why we did
not make our journey through Connemara on tricycles :
the roads are so good, the mail-cars offer such facili-
ties for the transport of baggage, the speed and sim-
plicity are so great.   To this we have our reply—
what then of the luncheon hamper ?   These ob-
jectors have not taken into account the comfortable
wayside halt by the picturesque and convenient lake ;
the unpacking of the spirit lamp, and its glittering
bride the tin kettle, the dinner knives at sixpence
apiece, the spoons at two-pence-halfpenny ; the potted meats, the Bath Olivers, the Bovril and the Bur-
gundy.   In the abstract we are not fond of picnics,
and agree with the Bard of " Ballads from *Punch* " in
thinking that—

> They who in contempt, the Dryad's haunts
> Profane with empty bottles and loose papers,
> Find tongues in tarts, ants running on their boots,
> Wasps in the wine, and salt in everything !

But a long road and an early breakfast create an
earnestness and sincerity in the matter of luncheon

that were lacking in the artificial junketings of the
Bard. Certainly, our stopping-places were not such
as a Dryad could haunt with any degree of comfort.
On this first day we pulled up under the lee of a low
bank, one of the few roadside fences we had come to
in that waste of heather and grey-blue lakes, and
spread out our eatables on the seats of the cart with a
kind of bashfulness of the possible passer-by ; a bashfulness soon to be hardened by custom into a brazen
contempt for even the passing. mail-car and the
fraternal backward grin of its driver. Most people
who have wolfed the furtive sandwich in a crowded
railway carriage have felt all of a sudden how gross
and animal was the action, but how, if persevered in,
a callous indifference may be attained ; this was the
case with us.

After that first lunch the complexion of things
changed. The wind sharpened into a wet whip, the
clouds swooped down on the hilltops, the lakes turned
a ruffled black, like a Spanish hen with its plumage
blown the wrong way, and the first mishap to the ex-

pedition occurred. I turned my head to look with
mild surprise at the end of an iron bedstead with which
an ingenious farmer had closed an opening in his stone
wall, and as I did so my hat soared upwards from

"WE PURSUED OUR WAY TO RECESS."

my head, and flew like a live thing towards the lake
by which we were driving. I followed with as much
speed as I possess, while my cousin lay in idiot
laughter in the cart, and had the pleasure of seeing

my hat plunge with the *élan* of a Marcus Curtius into
a bed of waterlilies by the bank.   From this I drew
it, pale, half-drowned, but sane and submissive ; and
placing it in solitary confinement at the bottom of the
trap, I donned a chilly knitted Tam o'Shanter, and we
pursued our way to Recess.

CHAPTER III.

DECOROUS black posts, with white tops, on either side of a little avenue, a five-pound trout laid out on the hall door-steps, with some smaller specimens of its kind, a group of anglers admiring these, and a fine, unostentatious rain that nobody paid any attention to—these were our first impressions of the Royal Hotel, Recess. With many injunctions as to her "giddiness" about the head, Sibbie was commended to the care of a stable-boy, and we marched over the corpses of the trout into a little hall in which the smell of wet waterproofs and fishing tackle reigned supreme.

Our only information as to the hotels of Connemara had been gathered from a gentleman whose experience dated some thirty years back. He told us that on arriving at the hotel to which fate had consigned him, his modest request for something more substantial than bread and whisky had been received with ill-concealed consternation. A forlorn hope of children was sent forth to find and hunt in a chicken for his dinner; he had watched the search, the chase, the out-manœuvring of the wily victim; he had heard, tempered by a single plank door, its death screech in the kitchen, and he had even gone the length of eating it, when it was at last served up on a kitchen plate, brown and shrivelled as "She" in her last moments, and boiled with a little hot water as its only sauce. As to the bedrooms, our friend had been almost more discouraging. He said that while he was dining he heard a trampling of feet and the moving of some heavy body in the passage. The door opened, and a feather bed bulged through the narrow doorway into the room, and was spread on the floor by the table. It was then explained that, as he had asked for dinner and a bed, sure there they were for him, and they were elegant clean feathers, and he should have them for eightpence a pound. With

some difficulty the traveller made them understand
that, though he meant to carry the dinner away with
him, he had no such intentions with regard to the
bed ; and after a more lucid setting forth of his
requirements, his host and hostess grasped the
position. He was taken into a
room which was quite filled by
two immense four-post beds, and
having been given to understand that one was reserved
for domestic requirements, he
was offered the other. He was
on the point of accepting this
couch when a snore arose from
its depths.

A FISHERMAN AT RECESS.

"Ah, sure, that's only the
priest," said the lady of the
house ; "and he's the qui'test man ever ye seen.
God bless him ! He'll not disturb ye at all." This
was our friend's experience, and though possibly it
had gained flavour and body with age, it had, at all

events, made us look forward with a fearful interest
to what might be our lot in Connemara.

But the first vision of the long Recess dinner-table
dissipated all our hopes of the comic squalor that is
endured gladly for the sake of its literary value, and
I may admit that the regret with which my cousin
and I affected to eat our soup and pursue our dinner
through its orderly five or six courses was not
altogether sincere. From one point of view it might
have been called a fish dinner, as from clear soup, to
raspberries one topic alone filled the mouths of the
diners—the outwitting of the wiles of trout and
salmon. There was a reading-party of Oxford men,
their blazers glowing rainbow-hued among the murky
shooting coats of the other diners ; there were young
curates, and middle-aged majors, and elderly gentlemen—to be an elderly gentleman amounts to a profession in itself—and all, without exception or inter-
mission, talked of fish and fishing. Not to talk to the
comrade of your travels at a *table d'hôte* is an
admission of failure and incapacity, so much so that

rather than sit silent, I would if need were, repeat portions of the Church Catechism to my friend in a low conversational voice. My cousin and I have seldom been forced to this extreme, and on this occasion we kept up the semblance of a cultured agreeability to one another in a manner that surprised ourselves. But the volume of discussion raging round us overwhelmed us in the end. We felt the Academy and the jennet to be alike an impertinence; we faltered and became silent.

Opposite to us sat one of the most whole-souled of the elderly gentlemen, with a face of the colour and glossy texture of Aspinall's Royal Mail red enamel, in vigorous conversation with a callow youth in a pink blazer, one of whose eyes was closed by midge-bites; and, though the general chorus might rise and wane in the long intervals between the courses, their strident bass and piping tenor sustained an unflagging duet.

"I assure you, my dear sir," protested the elderly gentleman, earnestly, with an almost pathetic oblivion

of the difference in age between him and his neigh-
bour, "it is not a matter of a fly with these Glendalough trout. I have seen a man fail repeatedly with
a certain butcher, and immediately afterwards the
same butcher, put *pleasantly* to a fish, you understand,
rose him at once."

"H'm," returned the Pink Blazer, gloomily, re-
ceiving this, to us, suprising statement, with perfect
calm, "*my* experience—and I've fished these lakes
for years—is that a full-bodied Jock Scott"—but we
will not betray our ignorance by trying to expound
second-hand the profundities of the Pink Blazer.
When they had been given to the world, he hid his
little midge-bitten face in a tumbler of shandygaff, while
his aged companion gravely continued the argument.

There were only two or three other ladies at the
table, and they evidently had, by long residence in
the hotel, been reduced to assuming an interest in
the prevailing topic, which we found hard to believe
was genuine. They may, of course, have been en-
thusiasts, but their looks belied them.

Next morning we were awakened by the babble of fishermen in the hall, then the rattle of cars on the gravel told that they had started on their daily business, and when at a subsequent period we came down to breakfast, we found ourselves alone, and the hotel generally in a state of peaceful lethargy. It was, so we had heard excited voices in the hall proclaiming, a splendid day for fishing. This meant that when we looked out of the window we saw two blurred shadows that we believed to be mountains, and heard the rushings of over-fed streams, which, thanks to the mist, were quite invisible. But the hotel weather-glass stood high, and at ten o'clock we were hopeful ; at eleven we were despairing ; at twelve we were reckless, and we went to our room to get ready for a walk. We have hitherto omitted all reference to one important item of our equipment, and even now, remembering that we were travelling in a proclaimed district, I mention with bated breath the fact that my second cousin insisted on taking an ancient and rusty revolver with her. She had secretly purchased a box of cartridges, weighing several pounds, and at the last moment she had requested me to stow this armoury in the travelling-bag—" In case of mad dogs and things on the road," she said. The pistol, in its leather case, I consented to, but the tin box of ammunition was intolerable, and we compromised by putting six cartridges into an " Easy Hair Curler" box, which really might have been made for them. So far there had been no occasion to use it, but now, as my cousin struggled into her mackintosh, she remarked tentatively, " Don't you think this would be a good day for the revolver ? "

I said I was not much of a judge, but she might bring it if she liked ; and having secreted it and a few " easy hair curlers " in her mackintosh pocket, she was ready for the road.

We paused in the hall for a last vengeful look at the barometer, which still stood cheerfully at Set Fair (we believe its constructor to have been a confirmed fisherman), and at the door we encountered the two hotel dogs—a large silky black creature of the breed that is generally selected to adorn penwipers, and a smirking fox-terrier, with polite, and even brilliant manners of a certain flashy hotel sort.

"Would they come for a walk with the ladies?"

THE TWO HOTEL DOGS.

said I, my voice assuming the peculiar drivelling tone supposed to be attractive to dogs.

The penwiper regarded me with cold amber eyes, and composed itself for slumber.

"Come along, then!" I said, still more persuasively adding, as I stepped out into the thick fine mist, "Cats!"

The amber eyes closed, and their owner curled into
an inky heap with a slumbrous growl ; while the fox-
terrier, having struck a dashing attitude to keep up
his character as a sportsman, affected to believe that
the cats I referred to were in the kitchen, and hurried
off in that direction.   We were snubbed ; and we
went forth reflecting on the demoralising effect of
hotel life.   Its ever-changing society and friendships
of an hour had turned the penwiper into an ill-man-
nered cynic, and the fox-terrier into an effete and
blasé loafer.   Thus moralising, we splashed along the
road, past the little post and telegraph office, where
you write your telegrams in an arbour of roses, and
post your letters between the sprays of clematis, and
struck gallantly forward, with the telegraph posts,
along the Clifden road.   Glendalough lake lay on our
left hand, and the bare mountains towered up on our
right—at least, we were given to understand by the
guide-books and the waiter that they towered, the
mist allowing us no opportunity of judging for ourselves.   Across the lake we saw the Glendalough

hotel among the woods that came down to the water's edge, and on it—we allude to the lake—were the boats of some of the maniacs who had left their comfortable asylum in the grey of the morning. We did not see them catching any fish ; in fact, we have been forced to the conclusion that we had some malign influence on the anglers of Connemara, for, though we have watched them long and often, we have never seen so much as a rise.

We left the main road at the end of the lake, and turned into one running in another direction. It was, like every Connemara road, good and level, and in perfect order. Like all the others, too, it disdained fence or protection of any kind, unless an occasional deep ditch or lake on each side can be called a re-assurance to the driver. Here and there on the road the little black demon cattle were standing disgustedly about, declining to eat the wet grass among the wetter heather, and concentrating all their attention on us in a manner that, taken in connection with the most villainous expression of countenance, and horns

like Malay Krisses, made it advisable to throw stones
at them while there was yet time. They at once
withdrew, recognising the fact that is early implanted
in the mind of every known Irish animal, that sermons
in stones are unanswerable. We had got on to a long
stretch of bog road, bounded only by the vaguely
suggestive mist, and we were beginning to feel the
ardour for a long walk awakening in us, when we
heard a strange yelping on the road behind us, and
looking back, saw a large brindled bulldog advancing
out of the mist at a lumbering trot. No one was with
him ; a short piece of rope hung round his collar, and
his aspect altogether was so terrific that my cousin
and I again provided ourselves with the national
weapon, and stood discreetly aside to let him pass.
He instantly stopped and stared at us in what seemed
a very threatening manner.

"Perhaps he's mad!" I suggested. "Where's the
gun ? "

"In my pocket," returned my cousin in a low voice
"and I can't get it out. It's stuck."

"NOW !"

"Well, you'd better hurry," I said, "for he's coming."

The bulldog was moving slowly towards us, uttering strange grunts, and looking excitedly round at the cattle, who were beginning to close in on us and him. My cousin with one strenuous effort ripped the pocket off her mackintosh.

"I've got it at last!" she panted, putting in a cartridge with trembling fingers and cocking the pistol. "It's awfully stiff, and I know it throws high, but anyhow, it will frighten him—I don't really want to hit him."

"For goodness' sake wait till I get behind you," I replied. "Now!"

There was a report like a cannon, and I saw my cousin's arm jerk heavenwards, as if hailing a cab. The next moment the cattle were flying to the four winds of heaven, and the bulldog, far from being alarmed or hurt, was streaking through the heather in hot pursuit of the largest cow of the herd.

This was a more appalling result than we could

possibly have anticipated. Not only had we failed to intimidate, but we had positively instigated him to crime.

" He's used to guns," I said. " He thinks we are cow-shooting."

" He's gone to retrieve the game," replied my cousin in a hollow voice.

In another instant the bulldog had overtaken his prey, and the next, our knees tottering under us with horror, we saw him swinging from her nose by his teeth, while her bellowings rent the skies. Back she came down the hill, flinging her head from side to side, while the bulldog adhered with limpet tenacity to her nose, and, jumping the bog-ditch like a hunter, she set off down the road, followed by a trumpeting host of friends and sympathisers who had re-gathered from the mountain-side on hearing her cries. The whole adventure had been forced upon us so suddenly and unexpectedly that we had no time to argue away the illogical feeling that we were responsible for the bulldog's iniquities. I see now that the sensible thing

would have been to have gone and hid about among
the rocks till it was all over.   But that course did not
occur to us till afterwards.   As a matter of fact, my
cousin crammed the pistol into her uninjured pocket,
I filled my hands with stones, and we pursued at our
best speed, seeing from time to time above the heaving backs and brandished tails of the galloping cattle
the dark body of the bulldog as he was swung into
the air over his victim's head.   Suddenly the whole
cortége wheeled, and flourished up a bohireen that led
to a cottage, and in the quick turn the cow fell on her
knees, and lay there exhausted, with the bulldog prone
beside her, exhausted too, but still holding on.   The
presumable owner of the cow arrived on the scene at
the same instant that we did.

" Call off yer dog !" he roared, in a fearful voice.

" He's not ours ! " we panted ; " but come on, and
we'll beat him off ! " the bulldog's evident state of
collapse encouraging us to this gallantry.

The man's only reply was to pick up a large stone,
and heave it at the dog.   It struck his brindled ribs

a resounding blow, but he was too much blown to bear malice satisfactorily; to our deep relief he crawled to his feet, slunk away past us on to the main road, and, setting off at a limping trot in the direction from which he had come, presently vanished into the mist.

The man stooped down and examined the poor cow's torn and bleeding nose, and she lay, wild-eyed, with heaving sides, at our feet.

" That the divil may blisther the man that owns him ! " he said ; " and if he isn't your dog, what call have you taking him out to be running my cows ? "

" We met him on the road," we protested. " We couldn't help his following us."

" Aha ! thin it's one of them dirty little fellows of officers that has the fishing lodge below that he be-longs to ! " said the man. " I heard a shot awhile ago, and ye may b'lieve me I'll have the law o' them."

We exchanged guilty glances.

" Yes ; I heard a shot, too," I said nervously.

" Well, I—a—I think we must be getting on now. It's getting late, and—a—I hope the cow isn't very bad. Anyhow "—my voice sinking into the indistinct mumble that usually accompanies the benefaction— " here's something to get soft food for her till her nose gets well."

The ambition for the long walk was dead. With more hurried good wishes and regrets we wished the man good evening, and so home, much shattered.

P.S.—We should like to meet the owner of that bulldog.

CHAPTER IV.

SIBBIE looked as suspicious and unamiable as ever
when she came to the door next morning; her
long day in the stable - had evidently not pro-
pitiated her in the least, but to her subtle mind had
only augured a journey of unprecedented length on
the following day. We started, however, with great
brilliancy, and with a vulgar semi-circular sweep, like
a shop-boy making a capital letter, that Sibbie considered very telling when in society. It took altogether
by surprise the penwiper dog, who, with a little more
than his usual elaborate ill-breeding, was standing
with his back to us, looking chillingly unconcerned,
and compelled him to show the most humiliating
adroitness in order to escape from Sibbie's venomous
fore-feet. The incident rounded off pleasingly our
last impressions of Recess, and we whirled out on to

the main road in a manner that nearly took our breath away, and probably left the gate-post in a state of hysterical gratitude at its escape.

It was not raining, but the day had got itself up to look as like rain as possible, and was having a great success in the part. A rough wind was blowing the clouds down about us, and, as on the day before, the hills hid their heads and shoulders in the odious mist, leaving only their steep sides visible, with the wrathful white watercourses scarring them, like perpendicular scratches on a slate. It was on one of these hills that a tourist missed his footing last year in trying to get to the bottom faster than someone else ; the heather clump broke from the edge of the ravine, and the young fellow went with it. They searched for him all the summer night, and next morning a shepherd found him, dead and mutilated, at the foot of the cliff. We drove on steadily by bare bog and rocky spur for three or four miles, with the wind hard in our faces, till we came to a cross road, where a double line of telegraph wires branched from the

single one, and following, according to directions
the double one, we left the mail-car road behind.
The wind now screamed into our right ears, and
Sibbie's long tasselled tail, which before had streamed
back out of sight under the cart, turned like a weather
cock and swept out in front of the left wheel. It was
not a pleasant day for seeing one of the show places
of Connemara, but it was the best and only one we
could afford ; besides, from what we had heard of
Ballinahinch, it seemed as if it would be able to
bear an unbecoming atmosphere better than most
places.

It need scarcely be said that the new road ran by
a lake, or lakes ; every road we have seen in Connemara makes for water like an otter, and finds it with
seeming ease, sometimes even succeeding in getting
into it. In a forlorn hollow by one of these lakes, we
came on a little Roman Catholic chapel, with its
broken windows boarded up, and its graveyard huddled under a few wind-worn trees on the hill behind.
Crooked wooden crosses, or even a single upright

stake, were the landmarks of the dead ; perhaps in a country where trees take more trouble to preserve than game, and are far more rare, a piece of timber is felt to be more honourable than the stone that lies profusely ready to the hand. The graveyard trees quivered rheumatically in the wind, long bending before it in one direction having stiffened them past waving ; the pale water chafed and sighed in a rushy creek below ; even Sibbie chafed and sighed as we stood still to look back, and she took at least ten yards of the hill at full gallop when we started her again.

As we drove along the high ground beyond, Ballinahinch came slowly into sight ; a long lake in a valley, a long line of wood skirting it, and finally, on a wooded height, the Castle, as it is called, a large modern house with a battlemented top, very gentlemanlike, and even handsome, but in no other way remarkable.

It was not the sort of thing we had expected. We had heard a great deal about Mary Martin, who was

called the Princess of Connemara forty years ago ;
we had read up a certain amount of Lever's " Martins
of Cro' Martin," of which she was the heroine, and
knew from other sources something of her gigantic
estate, of the ruin of it during the famine, of the way
in which she and her father completed that ruin by
borrowing money to help their starving tenants, and
of her tragic death, when she had lost everything, and
had left Ireland for ever.   We were prepared for anything, from an acre of gables and thatch to a twelfth
century tower with a dozen rooms one on top of the
other, and a kerne or a gallowglass looking out of every
window, but this admirable mansion with plate-glass
windows, and doubtless hot water to the very garrets,
shook down our sentimentalities like apples in autumn.
We drove on in silence.   I knew that my cousin felt
apologetic.

"I believe I had forgotten," she said, "that it
was Mary Martin's father who built this, sixty or
seventy years ago.   Of course you couldn't expect it
to look old."

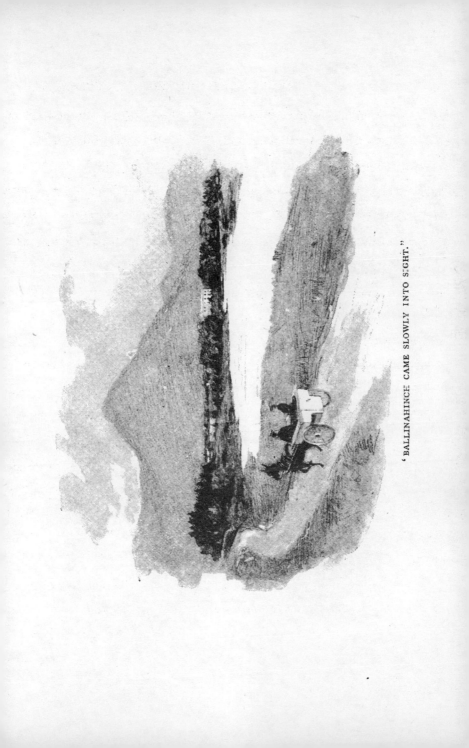

"BALLINAHINCH CAME SLOWLY INTO SIGHT."

"No, of course not," I replied, "and even if I did I don't think it would be much use. That house is too conscientious to look a day older than its age."

We arrived at the gate while I spoke, a modest entrance to what seemed a back road to the house, and Sibbie turned in at it with her usual alacrity in the matter of visiting. She would visit at a public-house, at a pigstye, at a roofless ruin, anywhere rather than go along the road. The picnic was beginning; certainly the view was. We looked along the lake and saw how it coiled and spread among its wooded islands; the shrouded hill behind it gave for the moment some indication of its greatness; there was no doubt that even at its worst, as it undoubtedly was, Ballinahinch was worth seeing.

The wind fought with us along the first stretch of the drive, dragging at our hat pins, lifting the rug off our knees; blowing our hair in our eyes; but at the first turning a great and sudden calm fell about us. For the first time in our travels we were in a large

plantation. Some local genius once said that "Connemara got a very wooded look since them telegraph
posts was put up in it," and after many a drive in
which the line of black posts dwindling to the horizon
was the only break in the barrenness we began to
understand this. Here at all events the civilising
hand had done its work, and we slackened pace in the
greenness and shelter, and, fortified by the know-
ledge that the present owner of the place was far away,
we began to think of luncheon. My cousin pacified
the fly-tormented Sibbie with a few handfuls of fresh
grass, and got out our pewter spoons and other ele-
gances of the luncheon table, while I, grovelling on
the floor of the cart, nurtured there the spirit-lamp
through one of its most implacable moods. There
was a charming stillness, broken only at first by the
occasional heavy splash of a leaping salmon in the
lake below, and by Sibbie's leisurely mastications,
then the first sulky sigh came from the tin kettle, and
a long beckoning finger of blue flame darted from
beneath it. That was a weird habit of the spirit-lamp,

to beckon to us when the kettle began to boil, and on
this occasion it did not play us false. We made our
homely cup of Bovril, we devoured our cheese, we
crunched our Bath olivers, and it was just then, when
the seats of the trap were covered with cups and
crumbs, and we were altogether at our grimiest, that
we heard wheels close at hand.

My cousin at once showed a tendency to get over
the wall and hide, leaving undivided degradation to
me, but the descent to the lake on the other side was
too steep. As she turned back discomforted I was
quite glad to see how dishevelled she looked, and how
crooked her hat was, and before any remedial steps
could be taken the Philistines were upon us. They
consisted of four young men, crowded on a car with
their fishing-rods and baskets, and, to do them justice,
they, after a first stare of astonishment, considerately
averted their eyes from the picnic. The narrowness
of the road made it necessary that they should pass
at a walk, and it was at that moment, while we were
affecting unconsciousness of all things in heaven and

earth, that the nightmare of yesterday rose up before us—the bulldog. He was close behind the axle of the car, fastened to it, thank heaven, with a glittering chain, but between the spokes of the wheel we saw his eyes rolling at us with a bloodshot amiability or even recognition, while his crooked tail wagged stiffly, and his terrible nose twitched amorously towards the Bath oliver I held in my hand. The car quickened up again, and he dragged at his chain as he was forced into a shuffling trot along with it. "Come in, Stripes," shouted one of the youths, and the party passed out of sight.

"Did you see him?" I said excitedly. "I believe he knew us!"

"Of course he did," returned my cousin, with an offensive coolness that was intended to carry off any recollections of her dastardly moment of panic, "but he won't tell. He knows if he gives us away about the revolver we will inform about the cow. For my part I'm rather sorry he isn't here now," she went on, as she wiped a knife in the grass, and then stabbed it

"WE HEARD WHEELS CLOSE AT HAND."

into the earth to give it a polish ; "no picnic should be without a dog. When I was a child we used always to wipe the knives on the dogs' backs between the courses at a picnic, and then the dogs used to try and lick that spot on their backs——"

I am not squeamish, but I checked my cousin's recital at this point, and we pursued our way to the house. Tall sliding doors, in perfect order, admitted us to a large quiet yard, so orderly that, as we looked round it, we felt, like Hans Andersen's black beetle, quite faint at the sight of so much cleanliness, and would have been revived by the only familiar whiff of the cow-shed and pigstye. We gave Sibbie and her luncheon bag to a man who was hanging about, and were proceeding to ask whether we might walk about the grounds, when a door into the house opened, and there issued from it a young woman of such colossal height and figure that we stared at her awe-struck. She smiled at us with all the benevolence of the giantess, and advancing, offered to be our guide. We thanked her like Sunday School children and followed her

meekly towards the hall door, feeling as we looked at
her that it would have been simpler to have climbed
on to her tremendous shoulders and got at once a
bird's-eye view of the demesne. It was apparently
part of the programme that we should see the inside
of the house, and she led us through the rooms in the
lower story, billiard-room, dining-room, drawing-room,
library ; all comfortable, and in their way imposing,
but unfortunately devoid of special objects to com-
ment on, while the giantess stood and held the door
of each open, with, as it seemed to us, an ogress-like
avidity for approbation. But she proved to be a
kindly giantess, and when we looked, in spite of ourselves, a little unenthusiastic at the prospect of view-
ing the upper part of the house she relented and said
we might go out into the grounds.

The hill sloped steeply from the dining-room windows, to the lake in front, and to a wood at the side,
and going down some steps we found ourselves in a
shady walk by the water.

" This is Miss Martin's seat," said the giantess, stop-

ping in front of a curiously-shaped and comfortless-
looking stone block, "ye can sit in it if ye like."

We did so, gently.

" How very nice," said my cousin, getting up again,
and removing an earwig and some dead leaves of last
year from her skirt, " but I should have thought she
would have liked more of a view. Those laurels two
yards off are very pretty of course, but one can't see
anything else."

I saw an antagonistic gleam in the giantess's eye
and hastened to suggest that the laurels might have
grown up since the days of Mary Martin.

" Whether or no, it's in it she used to sit," she said,
as if that settled the question of the view. " Maybe
ye'd like now to walk a piece in the woods to see
them ? "

" I suppose it would take us a long time to walk
through such large woods as these ? " I said lusciously,
seeing that I was regarded with more favour than my
cousin.

" Is it walk thim woods? Ye'd sleep, before ye'd

have them walked.   But there's a nice road round to
the boathouse ye can go."

"Perhaps you could tell me how many acres there
are in this estate?" said my cousin, trying to make
hay in my private streak of sunshine.

"I declare I'm not rightly sure."

"I suppose they're past counting?" continued my
cousin, with the fascinating smile of one who is sus-
taining a conversation brilliantly.

"About that," responded the giantess lucidly, determined at all hazards to keep pace with outside
opinion.   "Here now is the little road I was tellin' ye
of.   Would ye know the way in it?"

We assured her we could find the boathouse without her help, and "so in all love, we parted."

As we walked on in the solitude the lake narrowed
beside us to a river, a connecting channel between it
and the larger lake beyond, and the water ran strong
and quiet under the meeting branches that leaned
above it from both sides.   The dark mirror reflected
every twig ; brown stems, green canopy, and opening

of grey sky arched away beneath our feet as well as above our heads; we became at last giddy with the double world, and felt our eyes cling instinctively to the silver smear on the glassy surface or the golden gleam in the shallow that testified to where illusion began. Once or twice there was a splash that sounded, in that silence, as if a large stone had been thrown in; we were, of course, looking the wrong way each time, and instead of seeing the flash of a ten or twenty pound fish we saw only the rift in the crystal, and the big ripples following each other to the shore. Once only in Galway did we see live fish without stint or hindrance, when, afterwards, we leaned over the bridge in Galway town itself, and could have counted by the hundred the dark backs of the salmon that lie all day still and shadowy in the clear water below the weir.

We were soon out again by the upper lake, and, much beset by flies and midges, walked along the edge of the wood till we came to the boathouse. On its broad steps we sat thankfully down to rest, and

commented at our leisure on the atrocities of the grey
weather, and of the cloud that was cloaking the peak
of the mountain opposite. We happened to know
that there ought to be a mountain there, one of the
Twelve Pins, in fact, but for all we could see, it might
have flown into the Atlantic Ocean, in search of
something less watery than Connemara. As we sat
there, and saw the invariable fisherman catching the
inevitable nothing, and looked at the dark sheet of
water in its beautiful setting of trees, my cousin told
me drowsily several things about Mary Martin. I
cannot now recall the recital very clearly, but I remember hearing how Miss Martin had taken a guest
up the mountain that should have been soaring into
the heavens before us, and, making him look round
the tremendous horizon, had told him how everything
he could see belonged to her. If the weather had
been like ours, it would not have been a very over-
powering statement, limited, in fact, to the cloud of
mist and Miss Martin's umbrella ; but as it was, with
the inland mountains and moors clear to the bluest

distance, and the far Atlantic rounding her fifty miles of sea-coast, it was a boast worth making. Perhaps it was the vision that was clearest to her failing sense when she lay dying on the other side of that Atlantic without an acre and without an income, a refugee from the country where her forefathers had prospered during seven hundred years.

The retrospect became melancholy, and we began to be extremely chilly ; sitting out of doors was too severe a test for this July day, and we made towards the house again. When we were nearing Mary Martin's seat we saw through the trees a brilliant spot of colour, which gradually developed into a scarlet petticoat, worn shawl-wise about the head of an old woman who had sat down in a tattered heap to rest on the stone bench. She put away something like a black pipe as we came up, and began the usual beggar's groaning, and when, after some fumbling, my cousin produced a modest coin, the ready blessings were followed by the ready tears, that welled from hideously inflamed eyes, and trickled over the wrinkles in her yellow cheeks. It occurred to us to ask whether she remembered Mary Martin, and in a moment the tears stopped.

" Is it remember her ? " she said, wiping her eyes with some skill on a frayed corner of the red petti-coat. " I remember her as well as yerself that I'm looking at ! "

" What was she like in the face ? " said my cousin in her richest brogue.

" Oh musha ? Ye couldn't rightly say what was she like, she was that grand ! She was beautiful and white and charitable, only she had one snaggledy tooth in the front of her mouth. But what signifies that ? Faith, whin she was in it the ladies of Conne-mara might go undher the sod. 'Twas as good for thim. And afther all they say she died as silly as ye plase down in the County Mee-yo (Mayo), but there's more tells me she died back in Ameriky. Oh, glory be to God, thim was the times ! "

The tears began again, and she relapsed into the red petticoat. We left her there, huddled on the seat moaning and talking to herself. We could do no more for her than hope, as we looked back at her for the last time, that the pipe in her pocket had gone out. The day was slipping by ; a twelve mile drive to Letterfrack was before us. Taking all things into consideration, especially Sibbie's powers as a roadster, we hardened our hearts to starting at once, without taking the half-mile walk to see the wonderful stables that cost Colonel Martin £15,000 to build, and are paved with blocks of the green and white Connemara marble. Let us trust that our intended admiration was conveyed in some form to that costly marble flooring, in spite of an unpleasant saying about good intentions and a certain pavement that is their destination.

CHAPTER V.

IT was nearly four o'clock before we got out of the
Ballinahinch avenue on to the Clifden road. A
young horse had got loose in the yard just as
Sibbie was having her toilet made for the start, and
the clattering of hoofs and cracking of whips that
ensued had so upset her old-maidish sensibilities, that
she refused to leave the stable, till finally, by a noble
inspiration on our part, she was backed out of it.
She had started from the yard in a state of mingled
resentment and terror ; even still her ears were
fluttering like the wings of a butterfly, and she
showed a desire to canter that seemed to us unhealthy.
The shrunken oat bag lay at our feet ; decidedly she
had had more luncheon than was good for her while
we were walking ourselves off our legs in the woods of
Ballinahinch.   The broad lake lay on our left, show-

ing coldly and mysteriously through the changing
swathes of mist, and above us, on our left, the long
slopes of bog and heather stretched upwards till they
steepened into the dignity of actual mountains.

"If I thought the weather could not hear me,"
observed my second cousin, "I should say it was
going to clear up. It looks almost as if there were
sunlight on those children's petticoats ahead of us."
An enchanting group was advancing to meet us ;
half-a-dozen or so of children, boys and girls petti-
coated alike in mellow varieties of the dull red or
creamy white Galway flannel, a few cattle wandered
in front of them, and in their midst a long-suffering
donkey was being ridden by three of them and
beaten by the remainder. We were so absorbed in
sitting with our heads on one side to better appreciate
the artistic unity of the picture that we took no heed
of the dangerous forward slant of Sibbie's ears. No
one could have supposed that in her short intimacy
with "the quality" she could have already developed
a fine-ladyish affectation of horror at the sight of an

estimable poor relation ; yet so it was. Casting one
wild look at the appalling spectacle, she sprang side-
ways across the road, whirled the trap round, only
avoiding the black bog-ditch by a hair's breadth, and
fled at full speed in the direction from which she had
just come.

My cousin and I were for the moment paralysed by
surprise, and by the sudden horrid proximity of the
bog-ditch, which was hospitably prepared to take us
all in and do for us, and think nothing of it. Sibbie's
strong little brown back was hooped with venomous
speed, and her head was out of sight between her
forelegs. The telegraph posts were blended into a
black streak, the lakes swam past us like thoughts in
a dream, it seemed useless to get out to go to her
head ; obviously, Sibbie was running away. The
governess cart quite entered into the spirit of the
thing, and leaped and bounded along in a way that
—considering its age and profession—we thought
very unbecoming. It is perhaps a *façon de parler* to
say that I was driving. To put it more accurately, I

"HANGING ON EACH TO OUR REIN."

had been driving, and now I was trying very hard to do the opposite. However, after laying the seeds of two blisters in vain, I was ignominiously compelled to hand one rein to my cousin. Hanging on each to our rein, we lay back in the trap, getting a good leverage for our pull over the ridge of the luncheon basket. I shudder to think of the result had those reins broken. Two human catherine wheels would have been seen revolving rapidly over the stern of the governess-cart, and as for Sibbie—— But the reins were staunch, and though at first a want of unanimity caused us to swing from side to side of the road in a series of vandykes, the combined weight of the expedition slowly told, and Sibbie's ears were hauled into sight. Back and up they came till they were laid along her back, and her long nose pointed skywards in a fury of helpless protest, while her gallop grudgingly slackened.

Of course my hat had blown off early in the proceedings, but nothing else had happened. I handed my rein to my cousin without a word, and got out of the trap.

" No doubt this had been extremely amusing," I said, " but I am going to buckle the reins as low down on this bit as they will go."

And I did so. I hate people who do nothing but laugh on an emergency, simply because they think it looks brave.

As I turned Sibbie round I saw, nearly a quarter of a mile away, a child standing by a telegraph post, holding in its hand a white disc that I knew must be my hat, and I also saw with much pleasure that the other children, with the cows and the donkey, had left the road, and were climbing up the hillside. So, with hearts overflowing with a great thanksgiving that " Earl Percy," *i.e.*, the mail-car and its English tourists, had not " seen our fall," we drove back again at a cautious jog, Sibbie obviously as much on the look-out as we were for anything that she could reasonably shy at. The girl with the hat was regarded by her with an anguish of suspicion, only allayed by my getting out of the cart while the hat was smuggled in, and leading her—a process which always suggests taking a child by the hand to give it confidence.

It was a long way, about six Irish miles, back to the turn that we had been instructed would take us to Letterfrack, and the invalid sunshine had already swaddled itself again in cotton wool and retired for the night. If my second cousin has a failing, it is that she believes herself to possess "an eye for country," a gift fraught with peril to its possessor. Unfortunately, she had, before starting, studied on a map the relative positions of Ballinahinch, Recess, and Letterfrack, and now that she was face to face with the situation her eye for country flashed fire at the idea of having to traverse two sides of a triangle instead of one, which was pretty much what we were called upon to do.

"It is absurd," she said, hotly, "to go back almost to Recess to go by that 'new line' to Letterfrack, when I am almost *sure* I remember seeing on the Ordnance Map a dear little roadeen that would take us through the mountains somehow on to the Kylemore road."

From the use of the affectionate diminutive "roadeen," I knew that my cousin was trying to engage my sympathies, and though I tried to steel my heart against the suggestion, there certainly was something attractive in the thought of a short cut.

"It ought to be a little further on," she continued, "by a little lake ; and you know it's getting pretty late now."

I now recognise that this was the moment at which to have stamped upon the scheme, and to have made the time-honoured remark that we had no time for short cuts. But I let it slide by me, and when we reached a narrow, but to all appearance sufficient mountain road, bending plausibly away to the left, we mutually succumbed to its fascinations. For a mile or so it was really very fair. It certainly did occur to me that it might be awkward if we met anything larger than a wheelbarrow, as the governess-cart easily monopolised the space between the usual bog-ditches, but as, so far, the district seemed quite uninhabited, we did not trouble ourselves on that account. The

road became steeper and stonier as we advanced, but
Sibbie toiled on gallantly, the pride of having run
away clearly still working in her and encouraging her
in a way no mere whip could have done. The cotton-
wool into which the sun had retreated had now
covered all the sky, and was wrapping up the
mountain tops as if they were jewellery, which, as
they were armoured from head to foot in sheets of
grey rock, seemed to us unnecessary care. We were
getting deeper and deeper into the hills, and the
higher we got the heavier the rain became. It felt as
though some important heavenly pipe had burst, and
we were getting near the scene of the explosion. The
three shilling umbrella did its best; it humped its
back against the torrent like an old cab-horse, and
really kept my second cousin fairly dry. But things
were going very badly with the luncheon basket, and,
though we did not mention it to each other, the belief
in the short cut was dying in us.

The road ahead was narrowing in a way not to be
accounted for by the laws of perspective; it was

becoming suspiciously grassy, and rocks of a size usually met with only in the highest Druidical circles lay about so near to the track that steering was becoming a difficulty. A wild-looking women, wearing a coarse white flannel petticoat over her red hair instead of a cloak, came paddling along with barefooted indifference to the wet, and stopped to stare at us with a frank and open-mouthed amazement which was not reassuring.

" Shall we ask her the way ? " I suggested.

" It's no good," replied my cousin, sombrely ; " we must go on now. It's too narrow to turn round. Let's get on to those cottages and ask someone there."

(The belief in the short cut here heaved its final groan and expired.)

We had climbed to a kind of small plateau in the heart of the hills, and on the farther side of the little indigo lake round which the track wound were a couple of cottages. We beat Sibbie into a trot, and made for the nearer of the two, and the barking of the usual cur having brought a young man out of the house, my cousin proceeded to discourse him.

" Are we going right for Kylemore ? "

" Yo're not."

" Where does this road lead to ? "

"To the Widda Joyce's beyant."

" And is that the end of it ?   Can't we get on any farther ? "

The young man looked at us much as an early Roman might have regarded the Great Twin Brethren.

" Bedad I dunno what yerselves is able to do ; but there's no answerable road for a cart whatever "

Our eyes met in dumb despair, but my second cousin still rose above the waves.   (This metaphor is most appropriate, as we could not have been much wetter if we had been drowned.)

" Where is the nearest hotel ? " she asked, with all the severity of an examining Q.C.

" Back in Recess.   Ye'd be hard set to get there to-night."

" Think now, like a good boy, is there no sort of a place hereabouts where they'd put us up for the one night?"

The despairing relapse into the vernacular had its effect.

" Well, faith, I wouldn't say but the Widda Joyce 'd be apt to be able to do it.   There was an English gintleman, a Major, that she had there for the fishin'——"

In what capacity the English Major was used in the fishing we did not stop to inquire ; he might have been employed as a float for all we cared ; it was about all we felt ourselves fit for.

We did not ask the Widow Joyce if she could take us in.   We simply walked into her house and stayed there.   We had heard a good deal of the Spanish type of beauty that is said to abound in Connemara, but the Widow Joyce was the first specimen of it that we had seen.   A small, pale, refined woman, with large brown eyes, and dark hair tucked shiningly away under a snowy white frilled cap, she heard our story with flattering interest and compassion, and we had hardly finished it before most of her eleven children were started in different directions to prepare things for us and "the pony." By-the-bye, we noticed that during our travels Sibbie was always given brevet rank, the delicate inference being that we were far too refined and aristocratic to be associated with anything so vulgar as a jennet.

A lovely clear fire of turf was burning on the hearth, and Mrs. Joyce hospitably insisted on our each sitting on little stools inside the big fireplace, and roasting there, till the steam of our sacrifice showed how necessary a proceeding it was. In the meantime that sacred place known as "Back-in-the-room" was being prepared for our reception ; as far though we should have preferred the kitchen with its clean earth floor and blazing fire, Mrs. Joyce would not hear of our having our dinner there.

"Sure the Meejer always ate his vittles back in the room," she said ; and to this supreme precedent we found it necessary to conform.

We certainly owed a great deal to the Meejer. It was the Meejer, we discovered, who had broken an air-hole in the hermetically-sealed window. " An' faith, though he give us the money to put in the glass agin, we never got it done afther. It's a very backwards place here." The Meejer's sense of decorum had prescribed the muslin certains that shielded the interior from the rude gazer's eye. The Meejer had compelled the purchase of a jug and basin, and " a beautiful clane pair o' sheets, that not a one ever slep in but himself." In fact, what of civilisation there was, was due to his beneficent influence, and we rose up and said that the Meejer was blessed. Our dinner was an admirable meal ; a blend of the resources of the luncheon-basket and of Mrs. Joyce ; its only drawback being that, forgetful, as she herself admitted, of the precepts of the Meejer, she had put the teapot down " on the coals to dhraw," and the result was a liquid that would have instantly made me sick, and would have kept my second cousin awake in agony till she died next morning. So we avoided the tea.

"SITTING ON LITTLE STOOLS INSIDE THE BIG FIREPLACE."

" Back in the room " was a small whitewashed place with an earthern floor as clean, though not quite as dry, as the one in the kitchen. A big four-poster bed filled one end of it, and a red painted press, a square table, a huge American chest with the washing apparatus on it, and two or three chairs, were the rest of the furnishing. But though the upholstery was of a simple character, it was evident that the decorative sense was not lacking. The walls were lavishly hung with fervidly coloured religious prints ; two or three sheets of an illustrated fishing fly-list had a place of honour near the widow's patron saint over the fireplace, the gorgeous salmon flies being probably regarded by the younger Joyces as portraits of some new kind of angel ; and drapery's adventitious aid was lent by the suspended wardrobe of the family, both male and female, which relieved the severities of the bedposts, and gave a little air of interesting mystery to the corners of the room. Rather more than half the room had a rough ceiling of boards, and near the door we noticed a ladder leading up to the loft thus made. We had felt anxious about the bestowal of the widow and her family, not knowing what· duties the four-poster might not be called upon to perform, and as the witching hour of ten o'clock drew nigh, and the low murmur of Joyce discourse still continued, we had made up our minds to ask what the arrangements might be, when there came a tap at the door.

" I beg yer honour's pardon, Miss," said our hostess' soft, polite voice, " but would there be any harm in meself and the children goin' above up to the loft ? "

We said no, quite the contrary, and after some whispering and giggling outside the door, a procession of Joyces slowly filed up the ladder, headed by the younger sons of the house, and followed by the widow and the daughters. The last pair of stout red legs was hoisted off the ladder, the rustling and pounding overhead gradually subsided, and my second cousin and I found ourselves face to face with the most serious situation —not excepting either the bulldog or the runaway— of the expedition. The fear of interruption had hitherto prevented us from making as thorough investigation as we might have wished, and now we " stared at each other with a wild surmise, silent upon a peak in Darien." Then she said—

" I'll look."

She turned down the bedclothes with a stiff, nervous hand. " They seem pretty clean," she said at last ; " they mayn't perhaps have been washed very lately, but I think they must have dusted them. I can only see one crumb and a used wax match."

The account was not encouraging, but it might have been worse. Of the sufferings of that night, however, as much cannot be said. After our occupancy of that bed, not one used match, but twenty, might have been collected. In explanation of this circumstance, I will merely quote one line from the charming duet for bass and tenor in *The Lily of Kil-larney*—

To light the way, to flea my love.

CHAPTER VI.

FROM the indications given in the last chapter, the intelligent reader will probably have gathered the fact that we did not sleep well.

"It isn't the little bit they ates I begridges them," quoted my cousin, as in one of the long watches of the night she wearily lit her candle for the nineteenth time, "but 'tis the continial thramplin' they keeps up."

Even when the greater part of these foes was either gorged or slain, the sleep that hummed its mellow harmonies in the loft over our heads held far from us, tossing and stifling among feathers and flock pillows. It must have been about two a.m., and I had just, by various strategies, induced myself to go to sleep, when I was once more awakened, this time by a convulsive clutch of my arm.

"Don't stir!" whispered my second cousin, in a

voice so low that it felt like one of my own dreams, "but listen!"

A stealthy sound, as of a slow, barefooted advance, crept to us, buried though we were in the perfumed depths of the flock pillows.

"Whatever it is, it came out from under the bed," breathed my cousin, "and it has gone twice round the room—looking for our money, I expect!"

The steps ceased for a moment, then there came a sound as of a little rush towards the bed, and in an instant something with loud flappings and rustlings had descended upon us, and rested heavily, with hollow cacklings of contentment, upon our buried forms (for I suppose I need hardly state that we had both bolted under the bedclothes).

"I believe it's only the goose after all!" I said, as soon as I was sufficiently recovered to speak.

"Only the goose!" returned my second cousin, with concentrated fury; "I don't see much to be grateful for in that. And how do you know it isn't the gander? I'm simply stifling here, but I know the brute would peck me if I went out from under the clothes. I wish to goodness it *had* been a burglar. Anyhow, they don't peck."

This was indisputable ; as was also the fact that the bird had to be dislodged. She had worked herself into a position that was probably more satisfactory to her than it was to me, and judging, as I was well able to do, by her weight, she must have been a remarkably strong and vigorous bird.

" Get the matches ready," I said, gathering myself for an effort. Then, curving myself till the goose must have thought she was sitting on a camel, I gave a heaving plunge. There was a croak, a flop, and a minute afterwards the light of a match revealed a monstrous grey goose standing in pained astonishment on the floor near the bed.

Fortunately the profundities of Joyce repose knew no disturbance, and, still more providentially, the three shilling umbrella was within reach of the bed. Opening this as a safeguard against an attack, which in our then thin costume we should be ill-fitted to with-

"REVEALED A MONSTROUS GREY GOOSE."

stand, we gently but firmly ushered the majestic goose-lady into the kitchen, and, getting back to bed, slept in peace till the usual hideous farmhouse clamour began. We need not dilate upon it here. The war-whoopings of the cocks, the exhausting self-satisfaction of the hens over a feat which, however praiseworthy in itself, lacks originality; the yells of the pigs, and their impatient snuffings and bangings against the kitchen door; all, all, were alike detestable, and we welcomed almost with ecstasy the lowering of the first pair of Joyce legs, which told us that the family, like a certain distinguished cricketer, were going out " leg before."

My cousin and I are old travellers, and we have two properties, a spirit lamp and a folding india-rubber bath, without which we never take the road. It is my belief that if my second cousin were told that a chariot of fire was at the door, waiting to waft her to the skies, she would rush upstairs for the india-rubber bath and the spirit lamp. After this I suppose I need hardly say that they had accompanied

us to Connemara.   We do not for an instant wish to
insinuate that the bath, as an institution, does not ob-
tain in those parts.   We have every reason to believe
that it flourishes there ; but a melancholy experience
has taught us that the age of chivalry is dead, so far
as hotels are concerned, and if there is a scarcity or
competition in any department, whether of newspapers, or green peas, or baths, the most recent paper,
and the first helping, and the last available bath is reserved by the truckling domestics for the largely-
eating, heavily-tipping male traveller.   We have had
moments of fury, when violent death has stalked behind the chambermaid who has just informed us that
" the last bat' in the house is afther goin' in to the
gentleman in No. 11."

But at such times the remembrance of the india-
rubber bath floats sweetly into our minds ; and we
reflect that its tin rival would have cost sixpence or a
shilling.   Its gentle influence, combined with a dash
of chill penury, represses our noble rage, and we en-
dure the favouritism of the hotel *emlpoyés* with calm ;

knowing also that retribution is coming for her whose duty it will be to deal with the weird and wobbling thing that will, on the smallest provocation from the unskilled in its ways, become a mere mass of gaping mouths, pouring forth accusation of her and her treatment of the slightest visitor.

At the Widow Joyce's hot water was unexpectedly abundant, and the spirit lamp was not called into requisition. We were given to understand that the Meejer was loud and instant in his demands for "plenty of biled water," but how he performed his ablutions with it it is not for us to say. Except they lent him a churn, there was, so far as we could see, no vessels competent to undertake the duties of a bath, and a churn in such a capacity would, we should think, leave a good deal to be desired. We were, however, independent of such makeshifts. The chief drawback to an indiarubber bath is its propensity to slop ; but on an earthen floor slop is little accounted, and all would have been well if my second cousin had not persisted in trying to empty it through the air-

hole broken by the Meejer in the window. She did
this nominally out of kindness to the Widow Joyce,
but really because she thought she could pour its
contents on the widow's cat, who was sunning herself
on the window-sill. As a matter of fact, I think our
luncheon-basket suffered more than the cat—but we
will not pursue the subject. My cousin now recog-
nises that it requires an exceptionally high and hardy
intellect to control an indiarubber . bath, even in
repose, and few, very few, are able to direct it in
action.

When we went out that morning, we found it was
that " gift of God, a perfect day." Everything looked
washed and brilliant after the rain ; the little lake was
twinkling all over in sharp points of light till it looked
as if it were bristling with new pins, and the mountains had left off their half-mourning costumes of
black and grey, and wore charming confections of
softest green and lavender. We stood out in the
sunshine, on the narrow strip that ran between the
cottage and the lake, and threw some languid stones

at the widow's geese, who were bobbing along before
the wind, led on their voyage by the stout disturber
of our slumbers. The air was singing with the noise
of streams ; each pale blue ravine had a white line
dividing it ; at the back of the cottage a little overfed
river came foaming into the lake at a pace that ought
to have given it indigestion after all it had swallowed
the night before, and the plash of the contents of the
indiarubber bath, as the widow emptied it on the step
of the front door, gave the last note in the chord of
water-music.

We had had an excellent breakfast, founded on fresh
eggs and hot griddle cake, with a light top dressing of
potted meat ; we had paid our modest reckoning, and
Pat James, the eldest hope of the house of Joyce, was
harnessing " the pony." That " the pony " was giving
Pat James a time, not to say seven times and a half
time, was obvious from the shouts that came to us
through the stable-door, but finally, round the corner
of the cow-house, Sibbie's cross, prim face appeared
with Pat James leading her, and the governess-

cart reeling over the big ruts in the lane behind her.

" He's very crabbed, Miss," said Pat James, in tones of soft reproach, " he's afther hittin' me the divil's own puck inside in the stable."

There was a spiteful gleam in Sybylla's bright eye that spoke to the truth of his statement, and we felt sorry for Pat James.

We took a mutually affectionate farewell of the Widow Joyce, promising to convey her respects to the Meejer if we met him in England, as she seemed to think probable, and we set forth to make our way back to " the big road below," accompanied by Pat James, whose mother had charged him to see us safe over the first bad bit of the road.

He was an idyllically picturesque creature of seventeen or eighteen, with large, gentle grey eyes, set in a golden-brown face several shades darker in value than they were, and the most charming voice and manner imaginable.   The cat, on whom my cousin had basely tried to empty the bath, came with him ; sometimes strolling behind with a set face of unconsciousness, but with a tail that twitched with inward plottings, and sometimes making possessed scuttles on ahead, with a sort of squirrel's tail held high, and a little dreadful air of being moved by some unseen power. Pat James was evidently rather ashamed of it, and at such moments would throw stones at it to cover his confusion.

" We have it for a dog, Miss," he said in answer to our enquiries, " and it have the way now to be running with us when we'd be going out."

Here he threw another stone at the cat who had usurped the position of household dog, which had the effect of wafting it across the road under Sibbie's nose, and thereby alarming her seriously. He left us after about half a mile, and when we saw him last he was sitting on a big rock, his slouched felt hat and creamy flannel " bawneen " looking all that could be desired against their backgroundof clear blue sky, whilst the cat performed unearthly gambols in the heather at his bare feet.

"After all," we said to each other, as we turned into the main road, and set Sibbie's long nose for Recess, "it was just as well we missed our way, for if we hadn't we should have missed Pat James."

The road that was to be our portion was the one known as the New Line, leading out of the Recess and Clifden road into another road that leads through the Pass of Kylemore, and on into Letterfrack, where we meant to spend the night. Sibbie was fresh and full of going, and the long level road, following the curves of Lough Inagh and Lough Derryclare, inspired her with a fine and unusual zeal. The accustomed boats, each with its little patient whipping figure, were paddling about the lakes, and, according to our custom, we reined in the fiery Sibbie to watch them. They were a depressing spectacle, and, as usual, our cold, though anything but fishy, eye blighted all their chances of a rise. We left them all flogging away like Dublin cabdrivers, and made up our minds that if we wanted to spend thirty shillings a day on fish, we would do it at the Stores.

Our way lay through a long up-sloping tract of heathery, boggy valley, with the splendid towers and pinnacles of the Twelve Pins hanging high over the lakes on our left, and on our right the last outworks of the Maam Turc ranges rising almost from the road. It was an utterly lonely place. The small black-faced sheep pervaded the landscape, speckling the mountains like grains of rice, and we could see them filing along the ledges over purple depths where more than one climber has been killed. The little black and brindled cattle stared at us defiantly as we drove along, and the only human creature we met on the road was a grey old bagpiper, who looked as though he might have lost his way among the hills some time in the last century, and had only just found the New Line when we met him.

It certainly was a perfect day and a perfect drive. The delicious mountain wind, which was charged with all the subtle perfumes drawn from bog and heather ; the marvellous cloud effects on the great crags of the Twelve Pins ; the sparkle and rush of the brown streams under the innumerable hog-backed bridges ; the intense blue of the lakes, even the yellow whiteness of the slow-climbing road, all combined to fill us with that vague delightful yearning which can only be satisfied by lunch half an hour earlier than usual.

One only sign of civilisation did we see between Recess and Kylemore, and it was of a wholly unexpected type. A middle-sized house, bow-windowed, gabled, stucco-covered, hideous beyond compare, standing in the middle of a grass plot at the foot of one of the hills, and looking as if some vulgar-minded fairy had transported it bodily from Brixton or Clapham Rise. It had at first the effect of being deserted, but, as we got nearer, a melancholy old horse strayed out of a sort of dilapidated shed and stared at us, and an outside car propped against an elaborately gabled end showed that he was not a mere derelict. As we drove by, a cat climbed out of one broken pane of glass, and a cock crept in by another, and then suddenly at three of the upstair windows there appeared the faces of three dirty little girls. The hall door was shut, and the thin wiry grass round the house was untrampled. No other living thing appeared, and we can only conclude that we stumbled in upon the middle of a fairy tale. The house, of course, was the work of enchantment, and the three princesses, who were held there in durance vile, were about to be rescued by the princely cock whom we had seen forcing an entrance, while the bad fairy—the cat, naturally—had to creep out and throw up the sponge (of which, by-the-bye, the princesses might with advantage have made practical use).

We left the New Line just as we came in sight of the Pass of Kylemore, and the road on which we now found ourselves wound along the shore of the lake, according to the custom in Connemara, where, unlike the rest of Ireland, the roads are not planted along the backs of the highest hills procurable. We pulled up on one of the bends of the road to look at the view and make a sketch. That is the supremest of the advantages of driving your own donkey-cart, you can generally stop when and wherever you like. The only exception to this rule is when, as happened at Ballinahinch, your donkey has had too many oats.

On this occasion the donkey was quite ready to stop, and she surveyed, with a connoisseur's cold eye, the unsurpassable view, while the evening clouds thronged the gap between the steep tree-covered sides of Kylemore on one side, and the stony severities of the Diamond Mountain on the other, and sent changing lights and shadows hurrying over the wide lake, and drove the labouring sketcher of these things almost to madness.

Mr. Mitchell Henry's place, Kylemore Castle, stands close in among the woods under the side of Kylemore Mountain, with a small lake shutting it off from the road. It is a great, imposing grey mass of turrets and towers, and, close by, the white spire of a charming little limestone church is reflected among the trees in the lake, and gives an amazing finish of civilisation to the whole view—in fact, civilisation and fuchsia hedges are the leading notes from Kylemore to Letterfrack, wide crimson banks of fuchsia lining

MR. MITCHELL HENRY'S PLACE, KYLEMORE CASTLE.

the road, and prosperous farm buildings presiding over fat turnip fields, until the road lifts again into the barer uplands whereon is situated the village of Letterfrack.

No map we have as yet encountered pays Letterfrack the compliment of marking it, but it is nevertheless a very fine place, with a post and telegraph office, an industrial school, and a tolerably regular double row of houses of all sorts. Our various delays of luncheon and sketching, &c., along the road had made us later than usual, and we were only just in time for the *table d'hôte* at Mr. O'Grady's fuchsia-covered hotel. There was a wonderful sunset that evening, and after dinner we wandered out to see as much as we could before bedtime. It was the strangest country we had yet seen. A long down-sloping tract of semi-cultivated land, and, starting up round its outskirts, tall, crudely conical mountains, " such a landscape as a child would draw," my second cousin said. There was something volcanic and threatening about these great dark tents, showing awfully against the red background of the sunset. We were almost glad when everything melted into a grey sea-fog—for the sea, though out of sight, was very near—and we had to walk back the hotel ; while from a shadowy cottage back of the road the piercing screams of a concertina rendered in maddening iteration the first theme of the "Sweethearts" waltz. Only one incident did we meet with on our way back. Quite suddenly, out of the greyness, three men appeared, and as they passed us, one of them turned and said, "Genoong i dhieri," which, being translated, is "God speed you."

We said feebly "Good evening," and it was not till we were nearing the hotel that my second cousin remembered that she should have answered, "Ge moch hay ritth," which is the Irish method of saying, "The same to you."

CHAPTER VII.

THERE is reason in the roasting of eggs, and presumably in their poaching, but we are beginning to think we shall never fathom the principle which ordains that the hotel poached egg shall invariably be underdone. Charmed we never so wisely, commanded we never so timely, the same pinkish blobs were placed fluent and quaking before us, the same lavish gush answered the diffident knife puncture, and in a moment our plates became like sunrise painted by an impressionist, with red bacon streaks weltering in the widespread orange glories, and the golden mustard blob surmounting all as serenely as Phœbus Apollo.

This phenomenon was at all events our only specimen of a Letterfrack sunrise. As we sat at breakfast in the coffee-room the mist blew softly against the

French windows, and swept past on the road like a procession of ghostly ball dresses ; the furniture seemed clammy to the touch, and the paper decorations in the grate mocked the eye with their futile elegance and affectation of summer heat.   Our fellow guests, evidently *habitués* of the place, took only the most casual notice of the weather, and talked of local matters with the zest which so surprises the new-comer ; of their single or conglomerated prowess in scrambling up the Diamond mountain, of their tumbling down it, of their tea, their sandwiches, and their wet boots ; while we moodily ate our breakfasts, without even self-respect enough to make conversation for one another.   Our depression was deepened soon afterwards, on hearing that an ancient raw on Sibbie's shoulder had been touched by the collar in the drive of the day before, and that unless a person described as " Jack's father " could put some additional padding into the collar we could not get on to Renvyle that day, though it was only a four mile journey.

The prospect of a day spent in the coffee-room

and the little ladies' drawing-room goaded us to
energy. We determined to see the damage for ourselves, and putting on our waterproofs, we paddled
out into the yard, and picked our way across it to the
stable by some convenient and apparently recognised

JACK'S FATHER.

stepping-stones. The invalid Sibbie was in the dar-
kest stall of the stable, standing in severe pre-
occupation, with her back to the outer world, and as
we delicately approached her we became aware of an
eye like that of a murderess rolling at us with a white

gleam in the obscurity, and saw that her long, bell-rope tail was drawn tightly in. We hastily agreed that we would take Jack's word for the rubbed shoulder, and retired into the yard again. At the door of another stable we found the person whose only identity, or indeed profession, seemed to consist in being Jack's father, sitting on an upturned bucket, with Sibbie's collar in his lap and a monstrous needle in his hand. He explained that he was putting in a pad at each side, stuffed with cotton wool that he had got "from Herself, within in the house, because 'twould be kindher than the hay." He had a serious face, with a frill of grey beard, like a Presbyterian minister of the most amiable type, aud he looked up as he spoke with an expression that we felt to be kinder even than the cotton wool. "If that collar puts a hurt on the pony agin as long as yee'll be thravellin' Connemara, ye may—ye may call me blackbird!"

This handsome permission, emphasised by the tug with which the big needle was dragged through the leather, was evidently the highest reassurance known to the speaker, but, notwithstanding, we felt that even to apply the opprobrious name of blackbird to Jack's father would be an indifferent consolation if in the midst of a wilderness of moor and mountain we found the red spot appearing on Sibbie's shoulder. We looked, however, as properly impressed as we were able, and returned to the house in better spirits.

It was not till the afternoon that the weather gave us a chance of starting, and even then it required courage of a high order to turn out of our comfortable quarters into the thick, damp air. The volcanic mountain spikes, that last night had notched the sullen fire of the evening sky, had with one accord taken the veil, and retired from public observation, and the sloping pastures and turnip fields looked as nearly repulsive as was possible for them. Under these circumstances we left Letterfrack without emotion, and proceeded northward towards Renvyle.

After we had gone a little way we began to specu-late as to whether the road had been made with an eye to the possibility of a future switchback railway. It seemed to us that at every hundred yards or so we had to get out and trudge up a hill through the mud, our consciences approving our consideration for Sibbie, and our every other feeling bewailing it ; then came the scrambling into the trap again at the top, the tucking in of wet rugs, the difficult closing of the door, and having driven down the far side, the next hill rose immediately before us in the mist. The next thing we began to notice was that on every hill we met a donkey-cart and some young cattle, evidently coming from some fair or market. There were two courses of procedure on these occasions. The calves turned and fled before us at full gallop along the way they had come, until retrieved with huge expense of shouting and bad language, or they at once jumped the fence by the roadside and stampeded at large through the fields. The donkey-cart, which generally contained a pig, and an old woman screaming in Irish, had but one method, which was to cross to the wrong side of the road at the critical

AT TULLY FAIR.

moment, and then, abandoning itself to panic, en-deavour to retrace its steps. During three or four miles these *recontres* became more and more frequent, till at length, when the mist lifted at the top of a hill, we found that we had reached their source. In the hollow between the two hills was a village, its single street black with people, and the roads leading to it full of cattle and pigs. In other words, we had hit off the fair of Tully.

My cousin and I began to wonder how we were to get to the other side of it. We drove down into the town with dignity and circumspection, hoping that our aristocratic appearance might clear the way for us ; but after a minute or two we were forced to the conclusion that the peasantry were not impressed. Not till Sibbie's aggrieved visage was thrust into their midst did the groups separate, and even then they could scarcely spare time from the ardours of debate to give us more than a passing stare of bewilderment. An obstacle that seemed for a time likely to prevent our ever getting to Renvyle was a donkey-cart, with

its shafts propped on a barrel so as to make a stall
for the sale of sugar-stick, gooseberries, and piles of
the massive biscuits known as "crackers."   The press
of customers and their friends round this brought us
to a standstill, and my cousin, in a politely dignified
voice, asked those nearest us to move aside.   There
was a movement and a turning to stare.

"Holy Biddy! What's thim?" exclaimed a girl,
pushing back against the donkey-cart, and in so
doing sending some of the "crackers" sliding down
into the mud.

The proprietress, an old woman with protruding
teeth and generally terrific aspect, made a futile
attempt to avert the catastrophe, and then whirled
round upon us with a ferocity whetted by this disaster
and matured by long combat with small boys.

"That the divil may blisther yerself and thim!"
she screamed.   "What call have thim dirty thravellers
here throwin' down all before thim?   Aha! I knew
ye," she said, addressing herself to my second cousin
in tones of thunder, "and yer owld mother before ye,

the time ye were thravelling the counthry in a pack on her back, puckin' at every hall-doore in the counthry beggin' spuds! For so grand as ye are, with yer specs on yer nose and yer fine sailor hat on the back of yer head!"

My cousin and I should, of course, have passed on with a pale hauteur, as if we had not heard this amazing effort of biographical romance, but we are, unfortunately, not of the complexion that turns pale with ease; on the contrary, we became a violent turkey-cock scarlet, and ended by a collapse into unsuppressible laughter, in which the crowd joined with unfeigned delight, as they at length made a way for us to pass.

"Don't mind her at all, Miss," said a cattle drover, encouragingly, as he dragged a calf from before the wheel; "that one'd bother a rookery with her tongue; there isn't a fair in the counthry but she'll be bawling and fighting in it this way, so it's little regard the people pays to her and her chat. Sure, as Shakspeare says, "ye'll always know a rale lady wherever ye see her!"

This gallantry was so refreshing, that we did not stop to inquire more closely into the whereabouts of the quotation, and we slowly made our way out of the fair, past the bulging, grimy tents where porter and whisky were sold, and the screaming crowd of children in front of a showman's booth, till the last knot of blue-cloaked women was circumnavigated, and the last incensed pig was dragged from between Sibbie's forelegs.

We looked back as we crawled up the hill outside the village, and wondered what the pleasure could be of standing all day long in the drizzle, in mud ankle-deep, as many do who have nothing either to buy or sell. But a fair is not to them merely a place of business, it is a conversazione, extending from sunrise to sunset, at which the keen spectacular enjoyment of bargaining is blended with the purely personal pleasure of getting drunk.

Another mile or two of switchbacking brought us in sight of trees, which, in Connemara, answers to coming in sight of land, as far as civilisation is concerned; before long we were driving underneath them, and pulling up at the entrance gate of a demesne. We drove down a long avenue (when we say "avenue" in Ireland, we mean it according to the true sense of the word, and do not necessarily imply that it is over-arched with trees), with the sound of the sea in our ears, and became aware that we were on a strip of land like the battlefield of Lyonesse.

"On one side lay the ocean, and on one lay a great water."

We wound by the edge of the lake, and might easily have mistaken the frothy ripple along its shore for the salt lip of the tide, but for the tall band of reeds that shook stiffly in the mist-laden wind. But we were nearing the sea every moment. We emerged from a plantation, and came in sight of it at last, and at the same time came to our destination, a long, grey, two-storey house, with low Elizabethan windows, and pale weather-slated walls, wholly unexpected, and altogether unique, as far, at all events, as this part of Ireland is concerned.

Anyone who knows Galway at all, knows the name of Blake ; and anyone who read the reports of the Parnell Commission will remember the Mrs. Blake whose evidence there was thought by both sides to be of so remarkable a kind. Renvyle House, at whose oaken, iron-studded door Sibbie was now joyfully coming to a standstill, has been the home of the Blakes for several centuries ; now, in its old age, it is the home of any tourist who chooses to go there. The bad times and the agitation hit Renvyle very hard ; so hard that when the fight with the Land League was over, Mrs. Blake was not able to sit down and tranquilly enjoy her victory. She had, on the contrary, to rise up and give all her energies to repairing the ruin that such a victory meant. Her plan was a daring one for a boycotted woman to undertake ; but it was carried out to its fullest intention. Before long, advertisements appeared in the newspapers and the guide books to the effect that Renvyle House had been added to the list of Connemara hotels, and the sound of traffic, " the coorsing and

recoorsing "of cars began to be heard on the long
avenue by the lake, as in the old times, when "ex-
clusive dealing" and decrees of isolation were un-
known.

We cannot here say much about the difficulties she
had to contend with. Whatever they were they were
overcome. It is both easier and pleasanter to speak
of the advantages at her command. The charming,
rambling old house, with its innumerable panelled
bedrooms, the lakes, "shtiff" with brown trout, the
woods and rocks in which hide all manner of strange
beasts—from otters and seals downwards—the un-
tainted Atlantic for the tourist to disport himself in
or upon, as seems good to him, and the tallest mountains of Connemara to stare at across the bay, while
sprawling at ease on such a level, creamy stretch of
sand as is seldom found except in those places where
it is the sole and much-bragged-of attraction. We
had heard of all these things in advance; we were
accustomed to thinking of Renvyle as an hotel; and
yet, when we knocked at the door, and a grave and

decorous man-servant appeared, the look of every-thing conspired to make us forget that we were tourists, prepared to exercise our lawful right of " bed and board," and we came very near stammering out an inquiry if Mrs. Blake was at home.

CHAPTER VIII.

WHEN the iron-studded hall-door of Renvyle House Hotel had closed behind us, we found ourselves in a low-panelled hall, with oaken props for guns and fishing rods, and long black oaken chests along its walls. Everything was old-fashioned, even mediæval, dark, and comfortable. Nothing was in the least suggestive of a hotel, unless it might have been a row of letters and telegrams on the chimney-piece, and I was beginning seriously to fear that we had made a mistake, when I noticed my second cousin's eye-glasses were at full cock, and following their direction, I saw the "Innkeepers' Regulation "Act hanging framed on the wall. It was both a shock and a relief.

Our various belongings—somewhat disreputable and travel-stained by this time—having been conveyed from the trap, we were told that tea was ready in the drawing-room, and followed the servant through two deep doorways into another room, also mediæval and panelled. "What is so rare as a day in June?" asks Mr. Lowell. Nothing, we can confidently reply, except a fire in July, and there on the brick hearth we saw with gloating, incredulous eyes a heap of burning turf sending a warm, dry glow into the room, and making red reflections in the antique silver tea-service that was placed on a table near it. For ever quelled were our vague anticipations of the hotel drawing-room and its fetishes, the ornate mirrors, the glass-shaded clocks, and the alabaster chimney ornaments ; and as we extended our muddy boots to the blaze, and sipped hot tea through a heavy coating of cream, we felt reconciled to the loss of an ideal.

After the clank of our tea-cups had continued for a few minutes, there was a stir under the frilled petti-coat of the sofa, and a small black-and-tan head was put forth with an expression of modest but anxious

RENVYLE HOUSE HOTEL.

inquiry, the raised flounces making a poke bonnet round the face, and giving it an old-ladyish absurdity, of which its owner was happily unaware. We laughed —an unkindness which was followed by an expres-sion of deep but amiable embarrassment, and a tapping on the floor that told of deprecatory tail waggings. We simultaneously extended a piece of bread-and-butter, and an animal, allied apparently to the houses of black-and-tan terrier and dachshund, at once came forward with its best manner and took our offerings with suave good breeding and friend-liness. A trick of sitting up and waving the fore-paws as a request for food was exhibited to us with-out delay, and further researches discovered a pro-ficiency in that accomplishment of " trust" and " paid for," which must be the bitterest problem in dog-education, and perhaps gives in later dog-life some free-thinking ideas about the unpractical nature of the exercise, and the flippancy of supreme beings generally. We said all this to each other, luxuriously and at great length, and had some pleasure in con-trasting the refined behaviour of the Renvyle dog with the brutal cynicism of the Recess penwiper and the *blasé* effeteness of its fox-terrier. Under the influences of dark mahogany panelling and a low Queen Anne window we became mellow and thoughtful, and sank into soothing reflection on our natural affinity to what is cultured and artistic. I am sure, at least, that my second cousin felt like that ; she always has since the disastrous day on which a chiromantist looked at her hand and told her that it was essential to her to have nice surroundings.

I was beginning to feel a little acrid at this recollection when the door-handle turned in its place high up in the panels, and Mrs. Blake came in to see her visitors. That my cousin belonged to her county seemed to her a full and sufficient reason that she should welcome us as friends, and perhaps it gave us throughout our stay an advantage over the ordinary tourist in the more intimate kindnesses and opportunities for conversation that fell to our lot.

We looked as hard at Mrs. Blake as politeness would permit, while the broad columns of the *Times* seemed to rise before our mind's eye, with the story sprinkled down it through examination and cross-examination of what she had gone through in the first years of the agitation. It required an effort to imagine her, with her refined, intellectual face and delicate physique, taking a stick in her hand and going out day after day to drive off her land the trespassing cattle, sheep, and horses that were as regularly driven on to it again as soon as her back was turned. We did not say these things to Mrs. Blake, but we thought about them a good deal while we sat and talked to her, and noticed the worn look of her face and the anxious furrows above her benevolent brows.

It was some time before we went up to see the two rooms of which we had been offered a choice. Both were low and panelled, both had low, long windows ; in fact it will save trouble if we say at once that everything at Renvyle was long and low and panelled. The first room looked to the front of the house, and out over the Atlantic towards the muffled ghosts of Innis Boffin and Achill Islands; a fine view on a fine day, and impressive even at its worst ; but to us, the room's chiefest attraction was the four-poster bed, a magnificent kind of upper chamber, like a sumptuous private box, with gilded pillars, and carved work, and stretched canopy ; something to admire with the help of a catalogue at South Kensington. We felt, as we were taken down two long passages to view the other room, that it was a mere matter of form, and that the golden bed was too regal a circumstance to be abandoned. But before my cousin's eye-glasses were fairly adjusted for the inspection, we had begun to waver. The other bed was brass instead of gold, there was no denying that ; but these windows looked out to a great ridge of mountains, crowded about the head of the bay, roses climbed to the sill, and the grassy stretch below was cut out in gaudy flower-beds. A peacock screamed just under the windows, and we saw him with his meek spouse trailing his tail about the grass among the flower-beds that were wired in from his ravaging beak. I think it was the broad window seat in conjunction with the mountains that turned the scale—(the peacock also turned the scale, but in a different way, generally turning it at C in alt ; but, as Mr. Rudyard

Kipling says, that is another story). We forewent the golden glories of the new Jerusalem bed, and remained where we were.

There was unconfessed peace in the certainty that it was not an afternoon for sight-seeing ; rather for fervent shin-roasting at the drawing-room fire, blended with leisurely, unsystematic assimilation of the *Times* for the last four days. Fishermen, apparently, take a holiday from newspapers, along with their other duties when they go a-fishing, and expose themselves to nothing more severe in the way of literature than the *Field* or *Land and Water ;* at all events, these and a pre-historic *Illustrated London News* had been our only opportunities for keeping ourselves in touch with the outer world since we had left it. Boa-constrictor-like, we slowly gorged ourselves with solid facts, and then subsided into a ruminative torpor, misanthropically delighted at the fact that we had chanced upon an intermediate period as to tourists, and that the owners of the letters and telegrams that we had seen in the hall had not arrived to claim

' IT WAS THE BROAD WINDOW SEAT, IN CONJUNCTION WITH THE
MOUNTAINS, THAT TURNED THE SCALE."

them and their lawful share of the fire and the newspapers.

Our most salient recollections of the rest of the
evening are connected with the velvet delicacy of the
lobster soup at dinner, and the tortured bashfulness
of the English youth, who crept, mouse-like, into the
room after the rest of the
small party were seated,
and raised neither his eyes
nor his voice till the meal
was ended. Directly he
had finished, he hurried
from the room and was
seen no more. A lady
who sat next us volun-
teered the information

"SHE WAS AN AMERICAN LADY."

that he always acted just so, and that he spent his
days, so far as anyone could guess, in slinking around
the mountains. "He's so shy," she concluded, "that
he'll scrape a hole in his plate trying to get the last
mite of butter off it rather than ask me to pass

the cooler." It appeared that she was an American lady who had come to Renvyle to inquire into the advantages of the Land League and other kindred institutions, which was perhaps why she was in the habit of noticing little things. She certainly seemed to have noticed the Englishman a good deal.

Given a sloping, sunshiny bank of shingle, a mass of yellow lichen-covered rocks between it and a purple-and-emerald streaked sea, a large empty morning, and a cock-shot, there is no reason why one should ever stop throwing stones. That is how my second cousin and I occupied ourselves the morning after our arrival at Renvyle. We had started early, with sketching materials and luncheon, full of a high resolve to explore several miles of coastline, beginning with the famous Grace O'Malley's Castle, and ending with afternoon tea and well-earned repose.

No one can accuse these papers of a superfluity of local information. We have exercised a noble reticence in this respect, owing partly to a sympathetic dislike of being instructive, and partly also to the cir-

cumstance that we never seemed able to collect any
facts. We have questioned waiters, and found that
they came from Dublin, and bothered oldest inhabitants only to find that they were either deaf or " had
no English." But Grace O'Malley is a lady of too
pronounced a type to be ignored, and even our very
superficial acquaintance with her history compels us
at least to express our regret that such a female
suffragist as she would have made has been lost to
our century. If she had lived now she would have
stormed her way into the London County Council,
and sat upon that body in every sense of the word ;
and had the University of Oxford refused to allow
her to graduate as whatever she wished, she would
indubitably have sacked the town, and borne into
captivity all the flower of the Dons. In the reign of
Elizabeth, however, her energies were confined to the
more remunerative pursuit of piracy. She is known
to have had a husband, but he does not seem to
have occupied public attention to any extent, except
secondarily, as when it is recorded that " the Lady

Grace O'Malley went to England to make a treaty with the Queen, and took her husband with her." One of her strongholds was this square tower, that looks down with such amiable picturesqueness on the waters of Renvyle Bay, and we were told that on those rare occasions when she condescended to sleep ashore instead of afloat, a hawser leading from her ship was fastened to her bedpost, and the skipper had orders to haul on it if anything piratically promising should turn up.

I think we had begun to discuss this energetic Grace and her probable action in modern politics as we strolled across the fields between Renvyle and the sea. At all events, something beguiled us to sit down upon that slope of small round stones, when we were as yet but a quarter of a mile from the hotel, and then a flaunting tuft of white bladder campion on a point of yellow rock offered itself irresistibly as an object for stone-throwing. As we write this we are sensible of its disappointing vulgarity. The word "sketch," if not, indeed, "sonnet," should have closed the sentence;

but the humiliating fact remains that we simply lay there and pelted it till we had used up all the available pebbles, and stiffened our shoulders for the next three days, and still the bladder campion flaunted in our despite. We crawled from that too fascinating shingle beach to the grass above it, and stretched ourselves there in heated fractiousness. How hot the sun was! How blue and green the sea! And how enchantingly the purple gloom of the mountains showed between the grey hairy legs of the thistles! And after an interval of healing torpor, how admirable was luncheon!

But after luncheon Grace O'Malley's tower seemed farther off than ever, and relinquishing the vigorous projects of our morning start, we began to drift along the shore towards the pale stretches of the sands. We dawdled luxuriously across a low headland, where the mouths of the rabbit-burrows made yellow sandy patches in the coarse grass, and we slid down the crumbling slope on to the hard, perfect surface of the sand. Its creamy smoothness had something of the romance of new-fallen snow, and none of its horrors. An insane and infantine ardour possessed us—to run, to build castles, to paddle! We came very near paddling, forgetful of our age, our petticoats, and the fact that no one ever yet was able to paddle as deep as they wanted to. In fact, we resolved that we *would* paddle, and we set off down the slanting glistening plane towards the far-off line of foam. Here and there the blue sky lay reflected in the wet patches of sand, Achill Island was a cloudy possibility of the horizon, Croagh Patrick and Mweelrea, immense certainties of the north-eastern middle distance, and at our feet were laid lovely realities of long lace-like scarves of red seaweed, flattened out with such prim precision that we expected to find their Latin and English names written beneath them on the sand.

Another fifty yards would have brought us to the water's verge, when suddenly crossing our path at right angles, we came upon a long line of footmarks, masculine in size, pointed in shape, fraught with sinister suggestion of spying eyes. A group of immense rocks, the leaders of a procession of boulders trailing glacier-wise from the mountains to the sea, easily suggested an ambush, and the footmarks, as far as we could see, led in their direction. The same thought of the hidden watcher struck us both, and instantly and for ever abandoning the paddling scheme, we resolved to follow up the track of the footprints until we had routed the unworthy foot-printer from his lair. Little prods, as of a stick in the sand, accompanied the boot-marks, and at one spot certain rudimentary efforts in both art and literature made me think that the wearer of the boots was guiltless of object in his retreat upon the rocks. Suddenly, however, the marks lost their almost complacent evenness, and became extended and irregular, as if their owner had given himself over to ungoverned flight.

"What did I tell you?" remarked my cousin; "he was rushing off to hide before we should see him!"

We reached the rocks, and, with eyes that must have imparted to her *pince-nez* the destructive quality of burning glasses, my cousin swept their weedy crevices to discover some indication of the spy.

" He must be at the other side," she began, when our eyes simultaneously fell upon a small white object.

It was a sandwich.

It lay between two big rocks that leaned to each other, leaving just room for a slim person to squeeze through ; and looking through the aperture, we saw a long narrow vista of the sands, and on them a solitary flying speck—the Englishman.

CHAPTER IX.

THE sound of the mowing-machine awakened us early on the morning that we were to leave Renvyle House Hotel. To and fro the rattle came, with a measured crescendo and diminuendo that slowly aroused our sleepy minds to the consciousness that the tennis ground was being mown, and that it was Monday, and that—this finally, after sluggish eyes had become aware of pink roses swaying in sunshine in and out of the open window—another fine day had been bestowed upon us whereon to make our journey. The clatter of the mowing-machine grew louder, and the smell of the cut grass came in at the window, blending sweetly with the strong language of the gardener to his underling, as the machine was seered in its difficult course among the flower beds.

When we leaned out across the broad window sill, the business was almost finished, and the panniers of a donkey, who was standing on the gravel walk with his head drooped between his forelegs, in a half-doze

THE RENVYLE DONKEY.

were spilling over with the short green grass, and the chopped-off heads of the daisies. We stared at the donkey in a kind of bewilderment. The top of his head was tufted like a Houdan hen's, but stare as we might we could not see his ears, and it was so astonishing a phenomenon that we went downstairs to investigate it.

It was a genuine summer morning at last ; the sun shone hotly down on our bare heads as we passed the smooth lawn-tennis ground, with the long alternate grey and green lines ruled on it by the machine, and we stood for a moment or two in the shade of the thick fuchsia arch that led to the old-fashioned garden plot, and listened to the bees fussing in and out of the masses of blood-red blossom over our heads. The donkey was still dozing under his panniers as we came up to him, and we saw beyond any manner of doubting that the only ears he possessed were little circles no higher than napkin-rings, out of which sprouted thick tufts of wool and coarse brown hair. Just then the men neared us with the machine, and we asked them for an explanation.

" His ears was cut off in the time of th' agitation," the gardener replied, in a voice that showed that the fact had long ago ceased to have any interest for him, as he emptied the last boxful of grass into the panniers.

" He was a rale good little ass thim times, faith he was."

Probably our faces conveyed our feelings, for the gardener went on : " Indeed, it was a quare thing to do to him ; but, whatever, they got him one morning in the field with the two ears cut off him as even with his head as if ye thrimmed them with that mow-sheen."

We passed our hands over the mutilated stumps with a horror that evidently gratified the gardener. " There was one of the ears left hanging down when we got him," he proceeded.   " I suppose they thought it was the most way they could vex us.   They grewn what ye see since then, and no more, and the flies has him mad sometimes."

We went into breakfast with what appetite we might, and felt what terrible facts had conduced to the circumstance that we, tourists and strangers, were able to take our places in the old Renvyle dining-room, and partake of hot breakfast-cakes and coffee—coffee whose excellence alone was enough to make us forget we were in an hotel—as if we, and not the Blakes, had been its proprietors for centuries.

We spent the morning in making a final tour of the house, up and down the long passages, and in and out of the innumerable charming panelled rooms. We have left the library to the last, and now that we are face to face with the serious business of description, our consciences tell us that we are not competent to pronounce on ancient editions and choice bindings. It seemed to us that every book in the tall mahogany cases that stood like screens about the room was old and respectable enough to have been our great grand-father ; we certainly had in our hands a contemporary edition of Sir Walter Raleigh's " History of the World," not to mention an awful sixteenth century treatise on tortures, with illustrations that are still good, handy, reliable nightmares when the ordinary stock runs short. My second cousin has, I fancy, privately set up a reputation as a book-fancier, among people who do not know her well, on the strength of her graphic descriptions of one massive tome, a treatise on Spain, written in Latin, with gorgeous golden hieroglyphics stamped on its white vellum cover, and a date far back in 1500 on its yellow title-page.

I am sure that Sibbie felt small gratitude to the sulphate of zinc that brought about the complete healing of her sore shoulder, which took place during her visit at Renvyle. Probably never before since her entrance into society had she spent three whole days in a stable on terms of delightful equality with real horses, and with at least two feeds a day of real oats. " Beggars can't bear heat," is a tried and trusted saying in Ireland, and it soon became apparent that the moral and physical temperature in which Sibbie had been living had been too high for her. When we went to the hall-door to superintend the stowage of our effects in the governess-cart, we found her on her hind legs, with a stable-boy dangling from her bit, and flat on his back in front of her lay the respectable butler, overwhelmed in the rugs which he had brought out on his arm. We hastened to the rescue ;

the butler got up, Sibbie got down, and we proffered apologies for her misconduct.

"Oh, thin that one's the divil painted!" said the stable-boy, speaking, probably, on the principle of " Penny plain, tuppence coloured." " He went to ate the face off me to-day, an' I claning out his stall! Faith, 'twas hardly I had time to climb out over the side of the stall before he'd have me disthroyed."

The miscreant's appearance was that of a swollen sausage propped on hairpins, and, as having regretfully bade farewell to the hospitable house of Renvyle, we set off down the avenue at a showy canter, we promised ourselves that we would not strain the tender quality of mercy by any philanthropic nonsense of walking up hills.

Our route lay along our old acquaintance the switchback road for two or three miles, and then we said farewell to it, and turned to our left to follow the easterly line of the coast. It was not a bad little road in its way, but it was sufficient to chasten the exuberance of Sibbie's gaiety before we had travelled very

far along it ; in fact, as a midshipman observed of
Madeira, " The scenery was lovely, but very steep."
The coast thrust long rocky fingers into the sea, and
we drove across the highly-developed knuckles ; that
is, if notpicturesque, the most practical description
that we can give of this stage of our journey.   To try
to convey the blueness of the sea, the variety and
colour of the innumerable bays and creeks, the solemn
hugeness of Lettergash mountain that towered on our
right, is futility, and a weariness of the flesh.   Rather
let us speak of such things as we are able, of the dogs
whose onslaught from each successive cabin made it
advisable to keep a pile of stones in the trap, and
justified the time spent in practice at the bladder
campion ; of the London Pride and the great bell-
heather that ably decorated the rocks ; and, lastly,
the amenities of these are past.   This tract of country had a baneful practice of tempting us to pass by
a deferential retreat into the ditch, and of then instantly starting in emulous pursuit.   On one of these
occasions, after a stern-chase of half a mile, in despair

of otherwise putting an end to it, my cousin and I pulled up at a moderate hill, and got out and walked, hoping that the cart that had been clattering hard on our heels would now pass us by. Far otherwise; it also pulled up, and one of its many occupants called out in tones of genial politeness: "Ah! don't be sparin' him that way, ladies. He's well able to pull the pair of ye; nourish him wid the whip!"

Our destination was Leenane (pronounced Lee-nahn), but we had been advised to turn off the main road in order to see the Pass of Salruck. Slowly rounding the flank of Lettergash, we turned our backs to the sea and struck inland again into the now famiiar country of lake and heather. We had been told that a fishing-lodge by a lake would be a sign unto us that we had arrived at the by-road to Salruck. Here was the lake, and here the fishing-lodge; but could this be the by-road? If so, it certainly was not promising; in fact, before we committed our-selves to its stony ferocities, my cousin alighted in order to collect information from the peasantry, a task in which she believed herself to excel. In this instance the peasantry consisted of an elderly man, breaking stones by the side of the road, and the perspiring stare with which he received my cousin's question was not encouraging. She repeated it. He stared up at the sun, wrinkled his face till it looked like a brown paper parcel too tightly tied with string, and replied, " I'd say it'd be somewhere about a quarther behind three—or thereabouts."

" No," said my cousin in her shrillest tones, " I asked you whether that is the road to Salruck ? "

" Oh, it will—the day'll be fine, thank God," wiping his forehead with his sleeve, " but we'll have rain on it soon—to-morrow, or afther to-morrow. Ye couldn't put yer thumb bechuxt the shtarr and the moon lash' night, an' they'd reckon that a bad sign."

" Stone deaf," remarked my cousin to me in a " Just-Heaven-grant-me-patience" sort cf voice ; then, pointing towards the hill, " Is—Salruck—over— there ? " she slowly screamed.

The echoes squealed the inquiry from rock to rock.

Even Sibbie looked round with a cold surprise ; but the stonebreaker had not heard.

"Oh, is it *throut?*" in a tone of complete comprehension ; "Divil sich throuts in all Connemara as what's in that lake! Ye'd shtand in shnow to be looking at Capt'in Thompson whippin' them out of it!"

"Thank you," said my second cousin very politely ; "Good morning!"

We thought it better to chance the by-road than to try conversation. It was the first really bad road we had come upon in Connemara ; but, though there was only a mile of it, it was enough to throw discredit on the whole district. Half a mile of walking and of pushing the trap from behind brought us to the top of the hill, and when there an equally steep descent was in front of us before we could get down to the level of the little arrow-head shaped bay that thrust its long glittering spike between the mountains of Salruck. To hang on to the back of a trap as a kind of improvised drag is both exhausting and undignified, so much so that we did not drive quite down to the bottom of the valley, but paused on a perch of level ground outside the gates of a shooting-lodge, and asked a woman what the further road was like.

" Indeed, thin, God knows, it's a conthrairy road," she said, with a sympathetic glance at our heated faces, " but whether or no ye can go in it."

We thanked her, but made up our minds to throw ourselves on the kindness of the shooting-lodge, at whose gates we were standing ; and the trap and Sibbie having been hospitably given house room there, we were free to explore Salruck. We went down through a tunnel composed of about equal parts of trees and midges, and, following the conthrairy road over a bridge that crossed a little river, we sat ourselves down by the sea-shore and looked about us.

It may be said at once that Salruck is a place which would almost infallibly be described as " spot." A spot should be wooded, sheltered, sunk between mountains if possible, and, failing a river, a brook of respectable size should purl or babble into a piece of

"DOWN THE HILL OF SALRUCK."

water large enough to mirror the trees. A church is
not an absolute necessity, but is generally included in
the suite, and even down to this refinement Salruck was
thoroughly equipped. Having formulated this theory
to our satisfaction, we addressed ourselves to our
duties as tourists. We climbed the heathery Pass of
Salruck, a stiff windy climb ; we viewed from the top
of it the lovely harbour of the Killaries, and mountains and islands innumerable and unpronounceable ;
we came down again by a short cut suggested by my
cousin, of a nature that necessitated our advancing in
a sitting posture and with inconvenient rapidity down
a species of glacier. The pass happily accomplished,
we knew there was but one thing more to be done—
the graveyard. Our benefactors at the shooting-lodge
had told us how to find our way to it, and without
such help we certainly should not have discovered it.
It was hidden in the side of a wooded hill, a grassy
cart-track was its sole approach, a pile of branches in
a broken wall was its gate, and, instead of funereal
cypresses, tall ash trees and sycamores stood thickly

among the loose heaps of stones that marked the graves. At a first glance we might even have thought we had taken a wrong turn and strayed into a stony wood, but the kneeling figure of a woman told us that we had made no mistake. She got up as we came along the winding, trodden path among the trees, and we recognised her as the woman whom we had met on the hill an hour before.

" This is a quare place, ladies," she said in a loud, cheerful voice. " There's manny a one comes here from all sides of the world to see it."

We agreed that it was a queer place, and proceeded without delay into a long conversation. We found out that the high square mound of stones, about the height and length of a billiard-table, was an altar, in which only priests were buried ; and she pointed out to us under one of its stones some clay pipes and even a small heap of tobacco, which she told us had been left there by the last funeral for the use of "anyone that comes to say a prayer, like meself." In fact, all the graves were littered with broken pipes and empty boxes for holding the tobacco—grocery boxes most of them labelled with glowing announcements of Colman's Mustard and Reckitt's Blue, lying abou in all directions, and almost dreadful in their sordid garish poverty.

"There isn't one that dies from all round the counthry but they'll bury him here," said our friend, "and with all that's buried in it there's not a worrum, nor the likes of a worrum in it."

A little below where we were standing a circle of stones, like a rudimentary wall, stood round some specially sacred spot, and we stumbled over the ghastly inequalities of the ground towards it. Inside the stones the ground was bare and hard, like an earthern floor, and in the centre there was a small, round hole, with the gleam of water in it.

"That's the Holy Well of Salruck," said the woman, leaning comfortably against a great ash tree, one of whose largest limbs had been half torn from its trunk by lightning, and hung, white and stricken, above the little enclosure. "There'll be upwards of thirty sitting round it some nights prayin' till morning. It's reckoned a great cure for sore eyes." This with a compassionate glance towards my second cousin's *pince-nez*. "But what signifies this well towards the well that's out on the island beyond!" went on the country woman, hitching her shoulders into her cloak, and preparing to lead the way out of the graveyard; "sure the way it is with that well, if anny woman takes so much as a dhrop out of it the wather'll soak away out of it, ever, ever, till it's dhry as yer hand! Yes faith, that's as thrue as that God made little apples. Shure there was one time the priest's sisther wouldn't put as much delay on herself as while she'd be goin' over to the other spring that's in the island, and she dhrew as much wather from the holy well as'd wet her tay. I declare to ye, she wasn't back in the house before the well was dhry!"

She paused dramatically, and we supplied the necessary notes of admiration.

"Well, when the priest seen that," she went on, "he comminced to pray, and bit nor sup never crossed

THE HOLY WELL, SALRUCK.

his mouth for a night and a day but prayin'; there wasn't a saint in Heaven, big nor little, he didn't dhraw down on the head o' the same well. Afther that thin ag'in, he got his books, and he wint back in the room, and he was readin' within there till he was in a paspiration. Oh, faith! it's not known what he suffered first and last; but before night the wather was runnin' into the well the same as if ye'd be fillin' it out of a kettle, and it's in it ever and always since that time. The priest put a great pinance on the sisther, I'm told, but, in spite of all, he was bet by the fairies afther that till he was near killed, they were that jealous for the way he put the wather back. The curse o' the crows on thim midges!" she continued, with sudden fury, striking at the halo of gnats that surrounded her head as well as ours, "the divil sich an atin' ever I got."

We had been slaughtering them with unavailing frenzy for some time, and at the end of her story we fled from the graveyard, and made for the high-road.

The hospitalities of the shooting-lodge did not end with Sibbie.   Its hostess was waiting to meet the two strangers as they toiled, dishevelled and midge-bitten, to its gate, and with a most confiding kindness, brought them in and gave them the afternoon tea for which their souls yearned.

CHAPTER X.

WE have never met Julius Cæsar, or the Duke of Wellington, or General Booth, but we are convinced that not one of the three could boast a manner as martial or a soul as dauntless as the sporting curate on a holiday. We came to this conclusion slowly at the Leenane *table d'hôte,* and there also the companion idea occurred to us that in biting ferocity and headlong violence of behaviour the extra ginger-ale of temperance far exceeds the brandy-and-soda. Opposite to us sat three of them—not brandies-and-sodas—curates ; and our glasses were filled with two of them— not curates—bottles of ginger-ale ; and so the manners and customs of both classes were, as it were, forced upon us conjointly. If our reflections appear unreliable we are not prepared to defend them ; they were formed through the blinding mist of tears that followed each fiery sip of the ginger-ale.

The curates, as we have said, were three in number ; and comprised three of the leading types of their class —the dark and heavily moustached, the red-whiskered and pasty, the clean-shaven and athletic. The two former sat together and roystered on a pint of claret, which they warmed in the palms of their hands, and smacked their lips over with a reckless jollity and dark allusions to swashbuckling days at Cambridge. The third sat apart from his cloth, among a group of Oxford undergraduates, with whom he interchanged reminiscences, and from the elevation of his three terms seniority regaled them with tales of hair-breadth escapes from proctors and bulldogs, and, in especial, of the enormities of one Greene, of Pembroke, in con- nection with a breakfast given by a man who had been sent " a big cake from home." The story was long, and profusely decked with terms of the most

esoteric undergraduate slang, but we gathered that
Greene, having become what the curate leniently
termed "a little on," had cast the still uncut cake out
of the window at a policeman, upon the spike of
whose helmet it became impaled. We have since
heard with real regret that the Oxford police do
not wear spikes on their helmets; but we adhere to
the main facts of the story, and when we tell it ourselves we call the policeman a volunteer. The robust
voice of the narrator clove its way into the loud cur-
rent of the fishing talk, the table paused over its
gooseberry pie and custard to laugh, and even the
Cambridge curates were compelled to a compassionate
smile. They were a good deal older than any of the
Oxford clan, and it seemed to us that the superior
modernity and flavour of the Oxford stories had a
depressing effect upon them. They finished their
claret unostentatiously, and talked to each other in
lowered tones about pocket cameras and safety
bicycles.

It was strange to feel at this hotel—as, indeed, at all

the others we stayed at—that we were almost the only
representative of our country, and, casting our minds
back through the maze of English faces and the
Babel of English voices that had been the accom-
paniment of our meals for the last fortnight, two painful conclusions were forced on us—first, that the Irish
people have no money to tour with; second, that it was
Saxon influence and support alone that evoluted the
Connemara hotels from a primitive feather-bed and
chicken status alluded to in an earlier article.   Not,
indeed, that chickens are things of the past.   Daily
through Connemara rises the cry of myriad hens,
bereft of their infant broods, and in every hotel larder
"wretches hang that fishermen may dine."   Chickens
and small brown mutton, mutton and small brown
chickens—these, with salmon and trout of a curdy
freshness that London wats not of, were the *leit-motif*
of every hotel *table d'hôte*, and so uniformly excellent
were they that we asked for nothing more.

The whole of the next day was wet, utterly and
solidly wet.   The great mountains of Mayo on the

other side of the bay looked like elephants swathed
in white muslin, and the sea that came lashing up the
embankment in front of the hotel was thick and
muddy, and altogether ugly to look at. We sat dis-
mally in the ladies' drawing-room, with one resentful
eye on the rain, and the other fixed in still deeper
resentment on the wholly intolerable man who had
taken up his position in front of the fire with a book
the night before, and had, apparently, never stirred
since. From the smoking-room on the other side of
the hall came drearily at intervals the twanglings of a
banjo ; my second cousin read a hotel copy of " The
Pilgrim's Progress " ; the general misery was complete,
and I found myself almost mechanically working a
heavy shower into a sketch that had been made on a
fine day.

Towards evening we began to feel homicidal and
dangerous, and putting on our mackintoshes started
for a walk with a determination that found a savage
delight in getting its feet wet. No incident marked
that walk, unless the varying depths of puddles and

the strenuous clinging to an umbrella are incidents, but for all that we returned tranquillised and self-satisfied, and were further soothed by a cloudy vision caught, through the French window of the smoking-room, of blazers and white flannelled legs bestowed about the room in various attitudes of supine discontent. Before we sighted the window we had heard the melancholy metallic hiccupping of the banjo, but just as we passed by it ceased, and a furtive glance revealed the athletic curate, prone on a sofa, with his banjo propped upon the brilliant striped scarf that intervened between the clerical black serge coat and the uncanonical flannels.

> "Now the hand trails upon the viol string
>   That sobs, and the brown faces cease to sing,
>   Sad with the whole of pleasure. Whither stray
>   Their eyes now, from whose lips the slim pipes creep
>   And leave them pouting——"

misquoted my cousin, who has a slipshod acquaintance with Rossetti.

" I should think they strayed towards the Oughterard umbrella," I suggested, as we furled the tent of evil-smelling gingham in the hall. " Since the stuff has come away from two of the spikes it has got the dissipated charwoman look that is so attractive."

When we went to bed that night the rain was still dropping heavily from the eave-shoots, and, in the depressingly early waking that follows an early going to bed, it was the first sound that I recognised. The hotel was silent when we came down, and the coffee-room redolent of vanished breakfasts ; the fishermen had evidently betaken themselves to their trade in an access of despair. The waiter was reserved on the subject of the weather ; he neither blessed nor cursed, but hoped, with offensive cheerfulness, that it would improve, and we knew in our hearts that he was certain it would not. We watched him enviously as he came in and out with plates, and arranged long battalions of forks on a side table. What was the weather to him, with his house-shoes and evening clothes and absolute certainty of what he had to do next from now till bed-time ? We would thankfully have gone into the kitchen and proffered our services to the cook, or even to the boots, but instead of that we had to wander to the abhorred ladies' drawing-room, and there to mourn the fallacy of the statement that Satan finds some mischief still for idle hands to do.

It did clear up in the afternoon, grudgingly and gloomily, but still conscientiously, and we ordered out Sibbie, with a view to seeing how much of the country was left above water. We drove along the Westport road till we had passed the last long bend of the Killaries, and looking across a wooded valley saw the rush of water and jumble of foam above the mouth of the Erriff river that marked the chosen resort of the fishermen. We got a man to hold Sibbie for a few minutes while we went down and stood on the slender fishing bridge, and looked at a solitary angler throwing his fly with the usual scientific grace, and with the usual total absence of result, till we felt it would be kinder to go away. The midges were not perhaps as giant or as insatiable as the Salruck variety, but we heard that night at dinner that they had been enough to drive the whole body of the hotel fisher-men back from the river in the morning ; and as we looked down the double row of faces, all apparently in the first stage of convalescence after small-pox, we gathered some idea of what their sufferings must have been. One youth, whose midge-bites had reached the point at which they might almost be termed confluent, told us that he had lain down on the ground in a kind of frenzy and covered himself with his mackintosh, and that the midges had crawled in through the button-holes and devoured him as he lay.

We continued our drive towards Westport, with the river on one side, and on the other great green moun-tains speckled with thousands of sheep ; the road was steep, but we persevered up its long shining grey slope, without any definite intention except that of see-ing what was on the other side. We found out rather sooner than we had expected. There appeared sud-denly over the top of the hill, where the road bent its back against the sky, the capering figures of three young horses, and at that sight we turned Sibbie sharp round and fled down the hill. The young horses came galloping down after us with manes and tails flying, and visions of another runaway, with the final trampling of our fallen bodies by our pursuers, made us "nourish" Sibbie with the whip in a way that was scarcely necessary. She extended her long legs at a gallop; the trap swung from side to side; it seemed as if the horses gained nothing on us; and as the trees of Astleagh Lodge came nearer and nearer there flashed upon us in an instant the spectacle of a close finish at the hotel door, and the thought of the godsend that it would be to the smoking-room. But the smoking-room was fated not to behold it. As suddenly as the pursuit had begun so did it end. The three colts whirled up a bohireen towards a farmhouse, and we then became aware of a small girl running after them down the road with a stick in her hand. It was only the Connemara version of Mary calling the cattle home, written in rather faster time than is usual, and with a running accom-

paniment in two flats, supplied by ourselves. Sibbie
was not thoroughly reassured even when we reached
the hotel, and we drove past it along the road seaward
till we reached a point from which we saw the whole
of the long exquisite fiord of the Killaries, and
beyond the furthest of its dark, over-lapping points
the thin silver line of the open sea.

" Eight o'clock breakfast, please, and call us sharp
at seven," were our last words on our last night at
Leenane. The final day of our tour had come, and
two things remained imperatively for us to do. We
had to see Delphi, and we had to accomplish the
twenty Irish miles that lay between Sibbie and her
home in Oughterard. Energy and an early start were
necessary, and eight o'clock struck as we walked
into the breakfast-room, expecting to find our twin
breakfast-cups and plates stationed in lonely fellow-
ship at one end of a long desert of tablecloth. What
we did find was a gobbling, haranguing crowd of
fishermen, full of a daily, accustomed energy that
made ours seem a very forced and exotic growth.

The waiter, who at 9.30 yesterday morning had been servilely attentive, now regarded us with a coldly distraught eye. Clearly he was of the opinion of the indignant housemaid who declared that " there never was a rale lady that was out of her bed before nine in the morning." Breakfast after breakfast came in, but not for us. We saw with anguish the athletic curate make a clean sweep of the gooseberry jam, and the last of the hot cakes had disappeared before our coffee and chops were vouchsafed to us. Consequently it was a good deal later than we wanted it to be when we went down to the pier and got into the boat that was to take us across to Delphi.

The weather was grey and rough, and we asked the boatmen their opinion of it as we crept along in the shelter of the western shore of the bay, as close as possible to the seaweedy points of rock, the chosen playgrounds of the seals

" There's not much wind, but what there is is very high," said the stroke. " Faith, it's hardly we'll get

"EIGHT O'CLOCK BREAKFAST, PLEASE, AND
CALL US SHARP AT SEVEN."

over to Delphi with the surges that'll be in it when we'll be out in the big wather."

" Ah, *na boclish !*" struck in the bow, who, judging by his glowing complexion, was of the sanguine temperament. " I'd say it'll turn up a grand day yet. What signifies the surges that'll be in it ? "

We began to think it signified a good deal when, after a pull of nearly two miles, we forsook the shore, and, turning out into the open water, met the full and allied strength of the wind and tide. The " surges " were quite as large as any that we want to see, and the progress of the boat was like a succession of knight's moves at chess, two strokes towards the Delphi shore, and one stroke to bring her head to the advancing " surge." Naturally, we took a long time to get across, and when we got there we had still a walk of two miles before us ; only that it really did "turn up a grand day " our hearts would have failed us, as we felt the hours slipping from us, and remembered the journey that was before us in the afternoon.

Delphi was called so by some genius who saw in its

lake and overhanging mountains a resemblance to the
home of the oracle.   The boatmen were not able to
remember when the little lake had been converted
and rebaptized, or who the missionary had been, but
rumour pointed to a Bishop and a Dean of the Irish
Church, who, within the recollection of old inhabitants,
had been the first to impart civilisation to the Killaries ; who had built the charming fishing-lodge at
the head of the lake, and had fished its waters, attired
in poke bonnets and bottle-green veils.   We had not
been more than five minutes there before we understood the *rationale* of the bonnets and veils, and
wished that we had been similarly protected from
the blood-thirsty midges, that made our wanderings
by the lake and our lunch by the river a time of
torture.

But the stings of the midges have died away, and
the recollection of the glassy curve of the river, the
mirrored wild flowers at its brim, the classical grove
of pines and slender white birches, and the luminous
purple reflection of the mountain lying deep in the

stream beneath them are the things that come into
our minds when we think of our last day in Connemara. As a companion picture, belonging, too, to
that day, I seem still to see my cousin's sailor hat
flying from her head like a rocketing pheasant, in a
gust that caught us as we crossed the Killaries on our
return journey. It crested the "surges" gallantly for
a few minutes, but finally filled and sank with all
hands, that is to say, two most cherished hatpins,
before we could reach it.

That moment was the beginning of the end. One
of the most important members of the expedition
had left it, and the general dissolution was at hand.
The regret with which we paid our hotel bill was not
wholly mercenary, but was blended with the finer
pathos of farewell. The cup of bovril of which we
partook when the first five miles of our journey had
been accomplished was "strong as first love, and wild
with all regret"; it was the last of a staunch and
long-enduring little pot, and economy required that
no scraping of it should remain at the final unpacking

of the hamper. Gingerbread biscuits that had been hoarded like gold pieces were flung *en masse* to a passing tramp before even the preliminary blessing had flowed from her lips ; and the last of the seed-cake was forced into Sibbie's reluctant mouth. The frugalities of a fortnight were dissipated in one hour of joyless, obligatory debauch.

It was eight o'clock that evening when, after five or six hours' driving, we came down the long slope of the moor outside Oughterard. The mountains of Connemara were all behind us, in the pale distant guise in which we had first known them, and the only things that remained to us of our wanderings in their valleys were the governess-cart and the tired, but still dauntless, Sibbie. Even these would not be ours much longer ; the door of Murphy's hotel would soon witness our final separation, and to-morrow we should be, like any other tourists, swinging into Galway on the mail-car.

"Well, at all events," said my cousin, as we said these things to each other, "we have converted Sibbie.

"THE REGRET WITH WHICH WE PAID OUR HOTEL BILL WAS NOT
WHOLLY MERCENARY, BUT WAS BLENDED WITH THE FINER
PATHOS OF FAREWELL."

I have noticed several little things about her lately that make me sure she regards us with a stern affection. I daresay," she went on, " that she will detest going back to her old life and sur- roundings."

My second cousin looked pensively at Sibbie as she said this, and whipped up through the streets of Oughterard with a kind of melancholy flourish. Nothing was further from her expectations or from mine than the eel-like dive which, just as the sympa- thetic reflection was uttered, Sibbie made into the archway leading to Mr. Johnny Flanigan's stable ; and we have ever since regretted that, owing to our both having fallen on to the floor of the gover- ness-cart, Mr. Flanigan could not have credited the brilliant curve with which we entered his yard to our coachmanship. In fact, what he said was :

" Well, now, I'm afther waiting these two hours out in the sthreet the way I'd be before her to ketch her when she'd do that, and, may the divil admire me, but she picked the minnit I was back in the house for a coal to light me pipe, and she have me bet afther all.   But ye needn't say a word, when she hasn't the two o' ye desthroyed!"

FINIS.